ATTENTION RE

MW00450810

**To obtain your copy of the e-book/application that accompanies the hardcopy of this book, please complete the following steps:

1) *Email a copy of your receipt of purchase to: geschaffer@gmail.com*
2) *Title your email: "MTSS PROOF OF PURCHASE"*
3) *Receive your copy of the Nuts & Bolts e-book/application*

To learn more about preventative practices, provide a book review, obtain printouts, or report broken links, please visit:
http://geschaffer.wixsite.com/nutsandbolts

Schaffer, G. E. (2017). *Nuts and bolts: Multi-tiered systems of support: A basic guide to implementing preventative practice in our schools and community.* Albany, NY: New York Association of School Psychologists

To Dr. Lisa Kilanowski, Dr. Andrew Shanock, and the NYASP Board for your endless support and efforts. Thanks also to Mary Beth Pandolfino for her diligence as an assistant to the author and editors.

Special thank you to my parents for raising me to believe that anything is possible.

**To learn more about preventative practices, provide a book review, obtain printouts, or report broken links, please visit: *http://geschaffer.wixsite.com/nutsandbolts*

Schaffer, G. E. (2017). *Nuts and bolts: Multi-tiered systems of support: A basic guide to implementing preventative practice in our schools and community.* Albany, NY: New York Association of School Psychologists

Author Note

It's no surprise, systematic change from a reactionary refer-test-place model to that of a preventative three-tiered service delivery model is difficult! For those with much experience with Response to Intervention (RtI) to those with little experience, there are daunting challenges, alterations in educational roles, and a sense of urgency. Despite all the aforementioned factors, RtI has garnered considerable support across the nation for allocating resources more effectively, keeping educational funds replete, reducing special education rates, and providing a better opportunity than ever for students to succeed academically. For all these reasons and many more, RtI became law in NYS in 2012 and provided districts with set guidelines to follow. Unfortunately, RtI models implemented incorrectly or with little planning leads to seemingly insurmountable challenges, a sense of defeat, and confusion for even the most resilient of schools and organizations.

As a result, this manual has been developed to provide brief guidance, support, and proper implementation for not only RtI but for Multi-Tiered Systems of Support (MTSS). Under the Multi-Tiered Systems of Support model, the familiar three-tiered RtI triangle has been utilized to simply, unify, and delineate best evidence-based practices for attendance, academics (RtI), behavior (SWPBIS) social-emotional concerns (SWPBIS), and suicide prevention. Additionally, descriptions and set protocols for implementing intervention efforts have been suggested across the aforementioned areas. Together, we can all support one another in welcoming Multi-Tiered Systems of Support into our schools and make alterations to procedures as we learn and grow together.

Gary Schaffer
School Psychologist

***To learn more about preventative practices, provide a book review, obtain printouts or report broken links, please visit: *http://geschaffer.wixsite.com/nutsandbolts*

CLICK HERE TO PLAY VIDEO

CLICK HERE FOR AUTHOR BIOGRAPHY/CONTACT INFO

TABLE OF CONTENTS:

To learn more about preventative practices, provide a book review, obtain printouts, or report broken links, please visit:
http://geschaffer.wixsite.com/nutsandbolts

Introduction to MTSS

What are Multi-Tiered Systems of Support?

Multi-Tiered Systems of Support (MTSS) is an umbrella term utilized to describe triangular, multi-tiered intervention service delivery models. Central to MTSS models is that academic, behavioral, and social-emotional intervention efforts increase in intensity and duration for students who fail to respond to remediation (Averill & Rinaldi, 2011; Canter, Klotz, & Cowan, 2008). MTSS models are preventative in nature by providing struggling students immediate remediation in their areas of difficulty and offering educational staff set procedures and guidelines to assist students with learning, behavioral, and social-emotional difficulties (Averill & Rinaldi, 2011).

MTSS models diverge from traditional reactionary models of practice, such as refer-test-place special education procedures, in that they seek to remediate maladaptive learning, behavior, or social-emotional deficits before they lead to disability placement, school suspensions, or even criminal conduct (Averill & Rinaldi, 2011; Canter, 2008).

Arguably, the most well-known MTSS model is Response to Intervention (RtI). However, School-Wide Positive Behavior Support (SWPBS) has garnered considerable attention over the past decade for reducing office referral rates, school suspensions, and school expulsions. Although RtI and SWPBIS are the most common models that fall under the Multi-Tiered Systems of Support framework, deviations of these models have been developed by districts to promote uniformity across schools, abide by state guidelines, and provide early intervention to students with academic, social, emotional, and behavioral concerns.

In this book, five areas have been identified to promote academic achievement, pro-social behaviors, and emotional stability in the school environment. These five areas are: attendance, academics (RtI), behavior (SWPBIS), social-emotional well-being, and suicide prevention. Figure 2 provides a brief overview of the areas covered under MTSS and intervention service delivery models that accompany such models. Figure 3 on the following page provides a more detailed overview of MTSS and the frameworks that fall under the model.

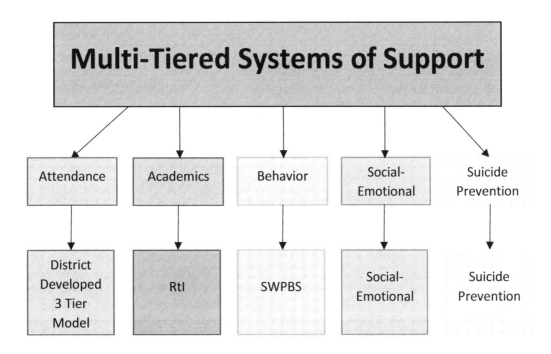

Figure 1

Multi-Tiered Systems of Support is a framework for providing systematic intervetnions and supports across the domains of attendance, academics, behavior, social-emotional, and suicide prevention/intervention. Through MTSS, schools can address students deficits and areas of difficulty early on to provide the child the best chance to succeed both in education and throughout their life.

The Three-Tiered Triangle: A Brief Overview

The traditional orientation of MTSS tiered triangles have been arranged with students needing the least support at the base of the triangle and needing the most support at the narrowest part of the triangle. At the base of the triangle, it is anticipated that approximately 80 to 85% of students will meet grade-level expectations and require no additional interventions. Students meeting grade level expectations and requiring minimal support are considered to be at the Tier I level of remediation efforts.

For those students who are not making adequate gains or meeting grade-level expectations, additional interventions are provided, such as small group instruction or replacement behavior training sessions. Approximately 10 – 15% of students will require interventions to remediate deficits and assist them in meeting proficiency in addition to Tier I support. Typically, students who receive small group support are considered to be at the Tier II level of remediation efforts/intervention. These students fall in the middle of the triangle.

Finally, at the narrowest part of the triangle, approximately 1 to 5% of students require intensive intervention in addition to Tier I support. These students are considered to be at the Tier III level of remediation efforts/intervention. Although multi-tiered systems of support have primarily been utilized as a means for developing evidence-based interventions, these models have long been cited an approach to assist in making eligibility determinations regarding special education (Gresham, 2005). Students who continue to display significant difficulties after receiving increasingly intense interventions may have a disability and may be eligible for special education services (Gresham, 2005)

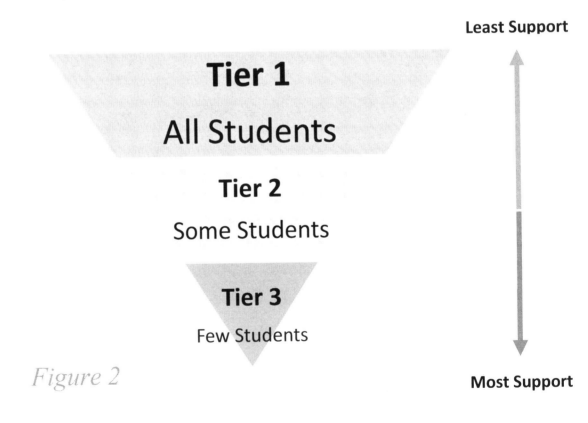

Figure 2

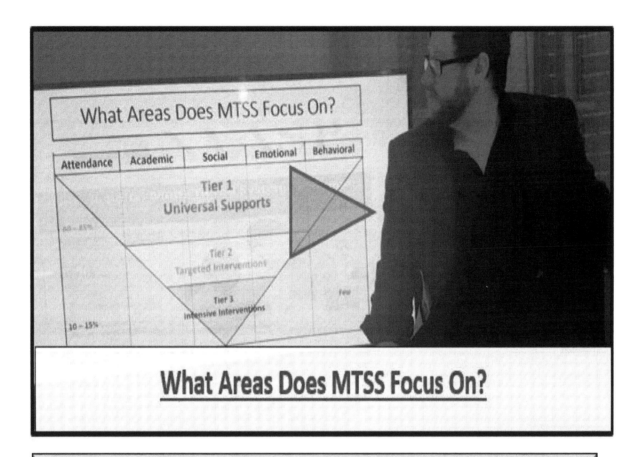

CLICK HERE TO PLAY WHAT AREAS DOES MTSS FOCUS ON VIDEO

General Commonalities Across MTSS Domains
For additional resources, please visit:
http://geschaffer.wixsite.com/nutsandbolts

Tiers	Attendance	Academics/RTI	Behavior/ SWPBIS	Social-Emotional	Suicide Prevention
Tier 1 (80 – 85% of Students) *Figure 3*	1. Educate parents, staff, and students on general expectations and policies in attendance, academics, & behavior. 2. Increase parents, staff, and students' awareness in social-emotional competency and suicide prevention. 3. Create a warm, welcoming, and caring school environment that fosters and values academic, behavioral, and social-emotional growth. 4. Universally screen all students and analyze data across each of the 5 domains. 5. Meet with child study team and school psychologist to determine best intervention options for students who are not responding to Tier 1 interventions. 6. Refer students who are not responding to Tier 1 intervention to receive Tier 2 support in their area(s) of deficit				
Tier 2 (20 – 25% of Students)	1. Re-teach key components of instruction, policy, and expectations 2. Provide supplemental interventions in push in or pull out small groups (3 – 6 students) 3. Intervention groups typically held 3 to 5 times per week for 30 – 45 minutes 4. Collect progress monitoring data on a weekly or bi-weekly basis (for RtI 12 – 14 data points recommended per intervention. 5. If student fails to respond to initial Tier 2 intervention efforts, meet with CST team to update on student progress and determine alternative Tier 2 intervention(s) to remediate area(s) of deficit 6. If all Tier 2 intervention efforts are exhausted, recommend child to receive tier 3 interventions!				
Tier 3 (1 – 5% of Students)	1. Provide intensive intervention through small group (2 – 3 students) or individualized instruction/support 2. Provide interventions 5 times per week for 30 to 45 minutes 3. Collect progress monitoring data on a weekly basis 4. In student fails to respond to initial Tier 3 intervention efforts, meet with CST to update on student progress and determine alternative Tier 3 intervention(s) to remediate area(s) of deficit 5. If all Tier 3 intervention efforts are exhausted, discuss with CST team recommending the child for special education services or, if attendance related, determine if outside assistance is needed (calling CPS, filing a PINS etc.) 6. Establish a wraparound continuum of care through working with the child and outside agencies/ clinicians to best provide services.				

© Gary Schaffer

Attendance

Why Attendance Matters?

Ask any teacher and they will tell you that students who are frequently absent from school are more likely to miss critical elements of instruction that help them build upon components already taught. An absenteeism report by Balfanz & Brynes (2012) revealed some alarming statistics regarding school absenteeism and adds further clout to educators' beliefs that students who frequently miss school are nothing for districts to "skip out on."

Balfanz & Brynes (2012) reveal that school absenteeism is frequently overlooked by districts because it is often not well tracked. In fact, it is estimated that 7.5 million students across the nation are chronically absent from school. Even more surprising is that schools can have an average daily attendance of 90 percent and evidence a chronic absenteeism rate of 40% (Balfanz & Brynes, 2012). According to Balfanz & Brynes (2012), chronic absenteeism is defined by students who have missed 10% or more of the school year for any reason.

Among elementary school children, chronic school absenteeism leads to students having to make up lost time which translates to lower achievement in 5th grade (Chronic Absence, n. d.). Still, 1 in 10 kindergarten students miss nearly a month of school every year and in some districts up to 1 in 3 kindergarten students miss class (Chronic Absence, n. d.). Students who are absent more than 10 days in an academic year are less likely to graduate high school and have a 25% lower chance of attending college (Balfanz & Byrnes, 2012).

In regards to skipping school, of the 500 secondary students interviewed for Balfanz and Brynes report, 75 percent indicated that they began skipping in middle and early high school. Ironically, more than 80% of students who skipped school once a week believed they would not fall behind their peers in class work (Balfanz & Byrnes, 2012). Secondary students' main reasons for skipping school were "boredom with coursework/school" (49%), followed by "more fun hanging out with friends" (44%) (GETSCHOOLED, 2012, p. 10). Results from Balfanz & Brynes (2012), Get Schooled (2012), and the Campaign for Grade-Level Reading (n.d.) strongly suggest that uniform district policies and procedures are needed to address chronic absenteeism and prevent future academic delay.

Due to students with chronic absenteeism tending to have lower grades and being less likely to graduate high school, an easy and simple guide is critical to increasing student attendance. Figure 4 shows a flowchart that to addresses school absenteeism. The flowchart uses the familiar three-tiered triangle from RtI/SWPBIS. The triangle has been developed to promote familiarity and provide easy guidance in addressing students who frequently miss school. For more information on preventing chronic absenteeism using a multi-tiered approach, the reader is directed to Attendance Works and Everyone Graduates' (2016) report entitled: **Preventing Missed Opportunity: Taking Collective Action to Confront Chronic Absence.**

"Reducing chronic absence requires a comprehensive, tiered approach that goes far beyond just enforcing school attendance rules" (Attendance Works, 2016, p. 5).

75% OF STUDENTS START SKIPPING IN MIDDLE SCHOOL OR EARLY HIGH SCHOOL

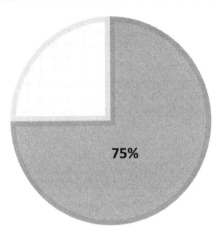

CLICK HERE TO PLAY ATTENDACE VIDEO

Attendance Flow Chart

Figure 4

For more on MTSS & attendance visit: http://www.attendanceworks.org/tools/schools/3-tiers-of-intervention/

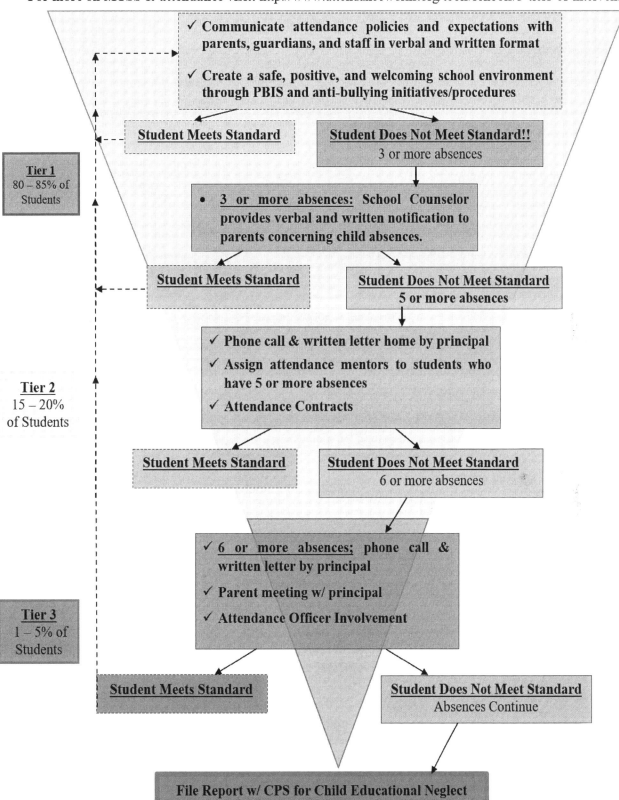

✓ Communicate attendance policies and expectations with parents, guardians, and staff in verbal and written format

✓ Create a safe, positive, and welcoming school environment through PBIS and anti-bullying initiatives/procedures

Student Meets Standard

Student Does Not Meet Standard!!
3 or more absences

Tier 1
80 – 85% of Students

• **3 or more absences:** School Counselor provides verbal and written notification to parents concerning child absences.

Student Meets Standard

Student Does Not Meet Standard
5 or more absences

✓ Phone call & written letter home by principal
✓ Assign attendance mentors to students who have 5 or more absences
✓ Attendance Contracts

Tier 2
15 – 20% of Students

Student Meets Standard

Student Does Not Meet Standard
6 or more absences

✓ **6 or more absences;** phone call & written letter by principal
✓ Parent meeting w/ principal
✓ Attendance Officer Involvement

Tier 3
1 – 5% of Students

Student Meets Standard

Student Does Not Meet Standard
Absences Continue

File Report w/ CPS for Child Educational Neglect

Resources & Interventions for Chronic Absenteeism:

Sample MTSS Attendance Triangle

Reducing chronic absence fits nicely into the three-tiered reforms systems used in many school districts and states. Tier I represents universal strategies to encourage good attendance for all students. Tier II provides early intervention for students who need more support to avoid chronic absence. Tier III offers intensive support for students facing the greatest challenges to getting to school.

Engaging Parents

BRINGING ATTENDANCE HOME
Engaging Parents in Preventing Chronic Absence

Attendance Toolkit

Count Us In!
Working Together To Show That Every School Day Matters

2014

Chronic Absence Calculator

G CHRONIC ABSENCE

Attendance Report

The Importance of Being in School:
A Report on Absenteeism in the Nation's Public Schools

Robert Balfanz
Vaughan Byrnes

May 2012

District Attendance Self-Assessment

Student Attendance Plan

MY CHILD'S ATTENDANCE GOALS

Teaching Attendance

Attendance Works   August 2014

Teaching Attendance:
Everyday Strategies to Help Teachers Improve Attendance and Raise Achievement

Attendance Counts

Attendance Counts!

ABSENCES ADD UP!

Response to Intervention

What is RTI?

Response to Intervention (RTI) is a three-tiered early intervention service delivery model that is part of the general education curriculum. RTI assigns students to tiers (e.g. Tier 1, Tier 2, and Tier 3) that increase in intensity and duration based on their lack of responsiveness to instruction at a prior level (Gresham, Reschly, & Shinn, 2010). RTI is based on the concept that universal screening, early identification, and early evidenced-based interventions can reduce and prevent future school failure (Gresham et al., 2010).

The ultimate goal of RTI is to avoid future delays which reduce overall academic achievement and possibly lead to placement in special education (Kilanowski, 2010a). Other goals of RTI include brining all students to proficiency, increasing the quality of general education programming and outcomes, avoiding the misclassification of students who have lapses in their knowledge as learning disabled, and ensuring that those students receiving special education services truly require that level of intensive academic support (Kilanowski, 2010a). Taken altogether, RTI follows the practices of: scientifically based instruction to replace weak intervention practices, universal screening to decrease the reliance on a flawed referral-based special education model, promotion of early identification and early intervention approaches in order to avoid the "wait to fail" approach, and progress monitoring (Gresham et al., 2010).

Through each of these practices, RTI has led to at-risk students being identified earlier, receiving services in a timely manner, being exposed to evidence-based interventions, and making more efficient use of limited resources (Gresham et al., 2010). In sum, RTI is a means of developing a more comprehensive and effective service delivery system that is based on "prevention, evidence-based interventions across tiers, data-based decision making, and early intervention that uses universal screening rather than referral" (Gresham et al., 2010, p. 8).

What do the RtI Tiers Look Like?

Tier 1:

Tier 1 services are delivered to all students in the general education classroom via the core curriculum and supplemental instruction. At this tier, differentiated instruction is provided to meet the needs of both strong and challenged students and is evidence-based (Kilanowski, 2010a). Differentiated instruction may be provided through the use of teacher directed centers or class-wide peer tutoring (Kilanowski, 2010a; Shinn & Walker, 2010). Moreover, Tier 1 intervention is provided by the general education classroom teacher during core literacy time. Although, instruction at this tier is evidence-based, it is less rigorous and intensive than at Tier 2 and Tier 3. Therefore, this tier may include both standard and non-standard protocol interventions (Kilanowski, 2010a).

As mentioned earlier, tier 1 involves universal screening for all students with up to 25% of students at this tier being progress-monitored and receiving more intensive intervention (Kilanowski, 2010a). This universal screening occurs typically in the fall, winter, and spring of each school year with data being used to plan for the instructional needs of all students and to decide if any students are in need of additional instructional support (at-risk). Students who are deemed at-risk in Tier 1 are referred for Tier 2 intervention.

In addition to being used to plan for instructional needs of students and determining students who are at-risk, data from universal screening is utilized to determine whether the school's academic programs are meeting the needs of most students. At this tier, approximately 80% of students should be achieving acceptable levels of proficiency (Kilanowski, 2010a). Evaluation of program fidelity/evidence base is necessary in the absence of this rate. Finally, examples of interventions for reading instruction at the Tier 1 level include timed repeated readings, duet readings, and Elkonin Sound Boxes.

Tier 2:

Tier 2 services are provided to students who may not have reached academic proficiency at the Tier 1 level. It involves supplemental programming in the regular classroom that can be either push-in or pull out (Kilanowski, 2010a). In this tier, intervention is both evidence-based and more intensive and rigorous than at tier 1. Therefore, supplemental intervention is delivered outside of the core curriculum and features standard protocol interventions. Standard Protocol interventions involve a program that is evidence-based such as Road to the Code or Great Leaps (Kilanowski, 2010a). Supplemental instruction at the Tier 2 level is delivered through the reading specialist or other individuals with appropriate training in intervention implementation and is typically provided to students in small groups. The recommendation for intervention at this tier is three to five times weekly for thirty to forty-five minutes. Moreover, this level of intervention intensity should last for a minimum of 12 weeks with progress monitoring data, featuring rate of improvement analysis (ROI) as the vehicle for determining more or less need (Kilanowski, 2010a).

In Tier 2, students are typically progress-monitored at least every other week (Kilanowski, 2010b). The data from progress monitoring at this tier is used to help a team form a hypothesis as to why a problem is occurring and to determine whether intervention has been effective. Students who do not respond to intervention at Tier 2 are considered to have severe and long-standing reading problems that cannot be remediated through interventions at the Tier 2 level and are referred onto receive Tier 3 intervention (Shinn & Walker, 2010). Students who do respond to intervention at the Tier 2 level are moved back into Tier 1. It is worthy to note that Tier 2 interventions are usually delivered to 5 to 10% of students.

Tier 3:

According to Shinn and Walker (2010), "Tier 3 is composed of intensive interventions for individual students with chronic or sever longstanding problems that exceed the capacity of Tier 1 or Tier 2 interventions to satisfactorily resolve their problems" (p. 6). In order to remediate these longstanding problems, tier 3 typically features highly structured standard protocol interventions that are delivered outside of the core instruction through pull out services. These interventions are typically delivered in exceedingly small groups via a reading specialist or another interventionist skilled in the target program) using principles of Direct Instruction (Kilanowski, 2010a). Intervention at Tier 3 is more intensive and rigorous than it is for Tier 1 and 2. Intervention at the Tier 3 level is recommended five days a week for thirty to forty-five minutes and lasts for a minimum fifteen weeks. It is important to underscore that student response to intervention as determined by rate of improvement analysis is the key to determining continued need and program modification. Students who respond to Tier 3 intervention are moved back into Tier 2 as opposed to students who do not respond to Tier 3 intervention and may ultimately be referred to receive special education services. Several cycles of intervention at both Tier 2 and Tier 3 may be necessary to determine student needs.

At Tier 3, progress is monitored at least once per week (Kilanowski, 2010b). Data from progress monitoring in this tier is used to identify students who are not progressing in reading at a rate high enough to close the achievement gap (Kilanowski, 2010a). *It is worthy to mention that Tier 3 is not special education and it typically consists of 1 to 5% of students.* Examples of Tier 3 intervention include the following: Reading Mastery, REWARDS, SRA Corrective Reading, or Wilson Language. Figure 5 on the following page provides an overview of the steps in proper RtI implementation. Figure 6 provides an overview of NYS Critical Elements to RtI.

NOTE: *Refer to the State of New York Education Department Response to Intervention: Guidance for NYS School Districts Handbook for intervention duration recommendations.*

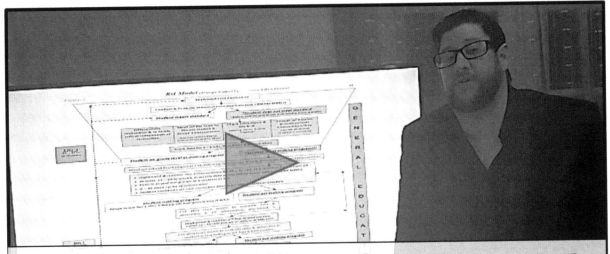

Commonalities of all MTSS Models, Deeper look at RtI, & Challenges to MTSS Implementation

CLICK HERE TO PLAY COMMONALITIES OF ALL MTSS MODELS VIDEO

How do MTSS Models Fail?

CLICK HERE TO PLAY HOW DO MTSS MODELS FAIL VIDEO

RtI Model (Triangle Flipped Upside Down-Like a Funnel); Figure 5

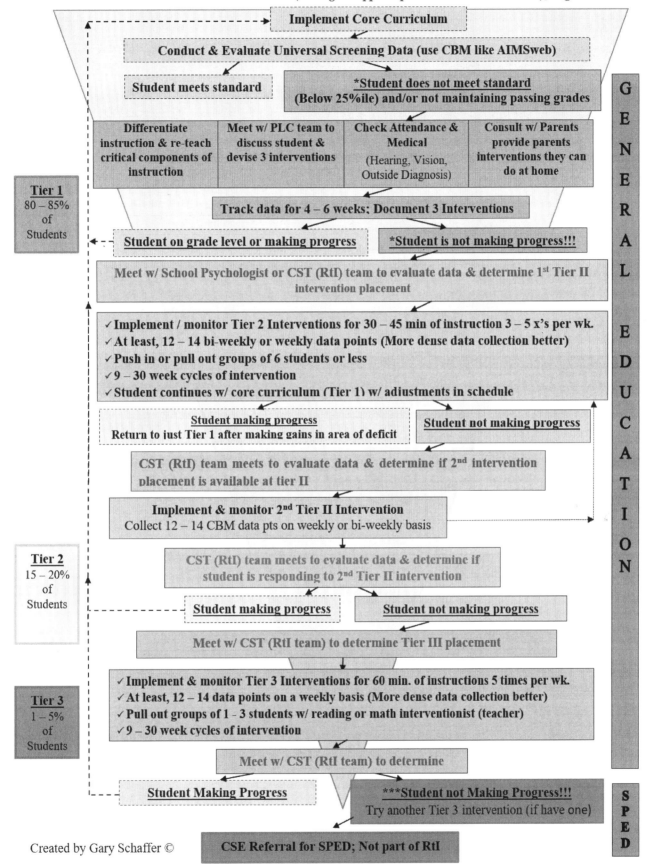

Created by Gary Schaffer ©

Table: NYS Description of Critical Elements in a 3-Tier RTI Model (Figure 6)

The following table was adapted from the *State of New York Education Department Response to Intervention: Guidance for NYS School Districts Handbook.* It outlines the essential features of a three-tiered model of RTI instruction suggested ranges of frequency and duration of screening, interventions, and progress monitoring per NYS. More information on RTI per NYS guidelines can be found here: http://www.p12.nysed.gov/biling/docs/RTIGuidance-Final11-10.pdf.

Adapted and reprinted with permission from Johnson, E., Mellard, D., Fuchs, D., McKnight, M. for NRCLD (2006, August) Responsiveness to Intervention (RtI): How to Do It.

Elements	Tier 1 Core Curriculum	Tier 2 Supplemental Instruction	Tier 3 Intensive Intervention
Size of instructional group	Whole class grouping	Small group instruction (3 – 6 students) **Generally recommended smaller groups for lower grade levels	Individualized or small group instruction (1 – 3 students) **Generally recommended smaller groups for lower grade levels
Mastery requirements of content	Relative to the cut points identified on DIBELS and continued growth as demonstrated by progress monitoring using DIBELS *CUT POINT: Lowest 25% of grade; grouped by areas of difficulty (i.e. DORF, LNF, CLS etc.)*	Relative to the cut points identified on criterion screening measures and continued growth as demonstrated by progress monitoring. Calculation of individualized goals and comparison of student's personal rate of improvement to that of national rate of improvement preferred.	Relative to the student's level of performance and continued growth as demonstrated by progress monitoring

Table: NYS Description of Critical Elements in a 3-Tier RTI Model;

The following table was adapted from the *State of New York Education Department Response to Intervention: Guidance for NYS School Districts Handbook*. It outlines the essential features of a three-tiered model of RTI instruction suggested ranges of frequency and duration of screening, interventions, and progress monitoring per NYS. More information on RTI per NYS guidelines can be found here: http://www.p12.nysed.gov/biling/docs/RTIGuidance-Final11-10.pdf.

Adapted and reprinted with permission from Johnson, E., Mellard, D., Fuchs, D., McKnight, M. for NRCLD (2006, August) Responsiveness to Intervention (RtI): How to Do It.

Elements	Tier 1 Core Curriculum	Tier 2 Supplemental Instruction	Tier 3 Intensive Intervention
Frequency of progress monitoring	Screening measures three times per year (i.e. CBM data; DIBELS, AIMSweb)	Varies, but no less than every two weeks.	Weekly
Frequency of Intervention Provided	Per school Schedule	Varies, but no less than three times per week for a minimum of 20 – 30 minutes per session Rec: 30 – 45 minutes; 3 – 5 times per wk.	Varies, but more frequently than Tier 2; Recommended 5 days per week; 60 minutes of instruction
Duration of Intervention	School Year	9 – 30 weeks	15 – 20 weeks
# of data points to move to next tier	**1** (in screening all students below 25th percentile move to tier 2 per grade level)	**12 – 14 (At least)** On a weekly or bi-weekly basis, at least 12 to 14 data points (On bi-weekly basis about 20 – 24 weeks into Tier 2 before moving to Tier 3)	**12 – 14 (At least)** On a weekly basis, at least 12 – 14 data points should be collected (or 12 – 14 weeks before moving to SPED recommendation)

NYS:

> *"A school district's process to determine if a student responds to scientific, research-based instruction shall include repeated assessments of student achievement which **should include curriculum-based measures** to determine if interventions are resulting in student progress toward age or grade level standards. [8NYCRR §100.2(ii) (1) (IV)]-NYS."*

What are Curriculum-Based Measures?

Curriculum-Based Measurements are brief, timed, and psychometrically sound probes given under standardized conditions that are comprised of basic readiness and academic material in the areas of reading, mathematics, spelling, and written expression (Kilanowski, 2010a; Shinn, 2010). CBMs are extremely sensitive to systematic change in learning basic critical components of instruction and are used to monitor student educational progress through direct assessment of academic skills (Wright, n. d.). The general time it takes to administer a CBM is 1 to 5 minutes (Wright, n. d.)

The child's performance on a CBM probe is scored for speed, fluency, and accuracy of performance. Since CBM probes are quick to administer, measure macro- and micro-skills, and simple to score, they can be given repeatedly (for example, twice per week) and are ideal for progress monitoring. After administering a CBM, the results are scored and charted to offer the instructor a visual record of a targeted child's rate of academic progress (ROI) and response to intervention (Wright, n. d.; Kilanowski, 2010b). A child's score is then compared to national and local norms and determines whether the student is at risk for not making acceptable gains in reading within the core curriculum. Figure 7 provides further information on CBM's

At the Tier 1 level of RTI, 25% of students can be progress monitored at one time and may also receive more intensive intervention (Shapiro, 2013). For those students who are at-risk (25% and below), more intensive intervention efforts are recommended. In terms of reading intervention screening and progress monitoring, the Dynamic Indicators of Basic Early Literacy Skills (DIBLES) and AIMSWEB are primarily used. Both these measures are standardized assessments that are relatively inexpensive and are quick to administer.

Special Note on Scholastic Reading Inventory from the National Center on Response to Intervention:

- *The SRI "has been evaluated for progress monitoring by the national center on response to intervention. However, recommended use is 3 to 4 times per year, so it is not appropriate for bi-weekly or weekly progress monitoring." (Schulte & Johnson, 2012).*

- *The SRI is considered a "computer adapted assessment" and not a CBM such as DIBELS or AIMSweb (Scholastic inc., 2012).*

- *Over 40 years of research supports the use of CBMs for progress monitoring!*

What are Computer Adaptive Tests?

Computer-adaptive tests (CATs) tend to be valid and reliable measures of broad academic concepts and applications and are designed to adapt to a students' ability level (Shapiro & Gebhardt, 2012). The test alters the selection of questions on the basis of a student's response ad provides a mechanism for identifying abilities and potential areas of academic deficit within the domain of the test. As the student responds correctly to an item, the test becomes progressively more difficult (Shaprio & Gebhardt, 2012). CAT measurement systems are administered to students on computers and are capable of examining a broad range of student skills. Test administration time can be as little as 10 to 15 minutes or as high as 1 hour. Examples of Computer-adaptive tests include the Scholastic Reading Inventory, Measures of Academic Progress (MAPS), and i-Ready.

Are Computer Adaptive Tests CMBs?

No. Computer adaptive tests (CATs) tend to measure broader academic skills and generally take longer to administer. Curriculum-based measures assess very basic readiness skills, components of instruction, and take less time to administer (Shapiro & Gebhardt, 2012; Shapiro, 2013). Although literature is growing on computer adaptive tests, curriculum-based measures continue to be the only *evidence-based* measurement system available in regards to universally screening and progress monitoring micro and macro skills acquired in instruction/intervention (Shapiro & Gebhardt, 2012; Shapiro, 2013).

Can Computer Adaptive Tests Be Used for Universal Screening & Progress Monitoring?

Yes and no. Although CATs show considerable promise for progress monitoring, there remains very little research supporting their use in such a manner. Additionally, due to computer adaptive assessments taking longer to administer than CBMs, they currently may be unrealistic in obtaining the 12 – 14 data points needed for reliable and valid decision making within an RtI framework and special education referrals (Shapiro, 2013; Christ, Zopluoglu, Monaghen, and Van Norman, 2013). Therefore, although CATs can measure a student's progress, the reliability, validity, sensitivity and feasibility of using these assessments for progress monitoring remains largely unknown. However, CBMs have well established evidenced-based support and are extremely sensitive in detecting slight changes in student learning (Fuchs & Deno, 1991, Kilanowski, 2010b, Shaprio, 2010).

When compared to CBMs, CATs may offer considerably more insight into student learning and intervention efforts. However, the "full evaluation of these measures in decision-making capability within an RtI model is still lacking literature" (Shapiro, 2013, p. 61). As a result, CBM's importance in measuring progress at the micro level remains a critical component in determining whether a student is responding to intervention. Figure 7 compares CMBs to CATs and other informal measures. For the time being, a combined approach of using computer adaptive assessments, curriculum-based measures, and other relevant academic data may provide the most accurate read as to whether a student is responding to intervention and reduce error in data-based decision team making (Ardoin & Christ, 2009; Shapiro, 2013).

Curriculum-based measurement (CBM) has been found to meet the criteria needed for effective universal screening (Shapiro & Gebhardt, 2013; Fuchs & Deno, 1991).

"STAR Early Literacy, Measures of Academic Progress, and the Scholastic Reading Inventory (SRI) all have the potential to serve in roles of effective progress monitoring metrics, although the full evaluation of these measures in decision-making capability within an RtI model is still lacking literature" (Shapiro, 2013, p. 61).

CBM VS Formal and Informal Measures (Figure 7)
Kilanowski, 2010

Curriculum-Based Measures	Formal and Informal Measures
DIBELS, AIMSweb, other CBMs: • Meet Ellis & Fout's evidence-based research standards (Over 40 years of research support CBM) • Measure micro & macro (higher order) skills • Allows for comparison to national and local norms • Scoring allows for determination of risk • Brief (1 – 8 minutes per probe) • Instrument is designed to be sensitive to small degrees of change/growth in student performance and psychometrically sound	*MAPS, IREADY, SRI, STAR PRGRAM, GATES, DRA:* • Many measures are have not met Ellis and Fout's evidence-based research standards • Designed to measure **_some_** micro skills more geared towards macro skills • Gates scoring allows for comparison to national norms but many other measures do not • DRA scoring references "absolutes" in terms of desired levels of performance not norm-referenced • Scoring allows for determination of risk • Not typically brief • Some instruments are not designed to be sensitive to small degrees of change

Curriculum-Based Measures	*Formal and Informal Measures*
• Research has found more accurate identification of struggling readers • Ideal to use for Progress monitoring • Can be administered many times throughout the year • Can be *relatively inexpensive* • Can be utilized to predict performance on state test using simple regression formula: $$Y = a + bX$$ *Y = Criterion being predicted (passing state test score)* *a = intercept of the two sets of data (the score on Y when X is 0)* *b = slop of the line that intersects the two sets of data* *X = independent variable (e.g., CBM-R score)*	• Some cannot be given repeatedly or if they can be given repeatedly; can only be given 3 to 4 times per year—not usable for progress monitoring • Tier 1 assessments may be conducted with less sensitive, but highly reliable computer-administered tools, such as the Measures of Academic Progress (MAPS) or STAR. May be hard to progress monitor using programs such as STAR due to the need for 12 – 14 weeks of data recommended to move from a Tier. STAR and Maps both longer measures! • Computerized assessments can *be relatively expensive* but offer much promise in *supporting and adding further validity to CBM. May be used as additive data for Pattern of Strengths and Weaknesses – pair with STAR, MAPS for best results!* Some CATS can be used to predict performance on state tests

What Data Is Needed for RtI & CST's?

NYS RtI Guidelines (2010) indicate that "the student-centered data collected and information on instructional strategies used throughout an RtI process provides important information to inform the CSE about the student's progress to meet age or state-approved grade-level standards (p. 20)." This data should include, but is not limited to:

- *Evaluative data,* including CBMs, regarding a student's performance

- *Progress monitoring data* that describes how a student responded to a particular interventions of increasing intensity

- *Instructional information* on a student's skill level and rate of learning relative to age/grade level standards or criterion-referenced benchmarks

Possible other sources of data
(NYS Guidelines, 2010 page, 20).

- *Grades*
- *Computer-Adaptive Tests Scores (CAT)*
- *State Test Scores*
- *Running Records*
- *Developmental Reading Assessment (DRA)*
- *Scholastic Reading Inventory (SRI)*
- *Common Formative Assessments (CFA)*
- *Common Summative Assessments (CSA)*
- *Psych. testing scores (if administered)*
- *Observation*

Each of the sources of data described above can be utilized to establish an academic *pattern of strengths and weaknesses (PSW)* in determining whether a student is at-risk for not meeting grade-level expectations. An academic pattern of strengths and weaknesses model utilizes various sources of data to obtain a unique profile of a student's specific strength and weakness across academic subject areas. Through using the PSW model, CST teams have a better understanding of what interventions the student may need and whether a specific biologically-based disability may be preventing a student from making academic gains. Should a biologically-based disability be suspected, completion of a PSW model involves a CSE referral and evaluation of the underlying cognitive processes that are preventing the child from responding to intervention (Naglieri, 2011). For a more comprehensive overview of evaluating cognitive deficits in determining the presence of a Specific Learning Disability, the reader is directed to Dr. Jack Naglieri's and Otero's (2017) work on the discrepancy/consistency approach to SLD identification using the PASS theory found in the book *Essentials of CAS2 Assessment* and Naglieri's past work using the Cognitive Assessment System (CAS & CAS-2). Figure 8 provides a diagram of an established academic PSW on a student who is not progressing in reading.

Academic PSW Model Sample

Grade 4	Measure of Assessment			
Subject	*CBM*	Grades	CAT STAR, MAPS	State Test
Math	60 (Met)	B	220 (Proficient)	Level 2 (Met Basic)
Reading	61 At-Risk	D	475 Emergent	Level 1 (Well-Below)
Writing	65 (Above Benchmark)	A	275 (Proficient)	Level 4 (Established)

Strength   **At-Risk**   **Weakness**   *Figure 8*

"An academic pattern of strengths and weaknesses model utilizes various sources of data to obtain a unique profile of a student's specific strength and weakness across academic subject areas. Through using the PSW model, CST teams have a better understanding of what interventions the student may need and whether a specific biologically-based disability may be preventing a student from making academic gains."

Patterns of Strengths & Weaknesses Model in Specific Learning Disability Assessment

Dr. John Garruto
Co-Author: Essentials of WJ-IV Cog. Abilities Assessment

CLICK HERE TO PLAY PSW VIDEO

How Long Should Data Collection Occur?

Although many districts still utilize the past practice of collecting 6 to 8 data points per intervention, such sparse data collection is likely to result in invalid and unreliable educational decision in regards to intervention implementation and whether to refer a child to special education. Recently, Christ et al., (2013) revealed that 12 – 14 weeks of data may provide educators with more valid and reliable data in the decision making process. In the case where data is collected on a weekly basis across Tier II and Tier III, at least 24 to 28 total data points (24 – 28 weeks) is suggested before recommending a student for special education testing (Christ et al., 2013; Shapiro, 2013). An additional 12 – 14 weeks of data would have to be collected if another intervention was implemented.

Why So Much Data and Why So Long?

Often teachers and administrators worry about whether we are "waiting too long" for the data collection process to take place. The concern stems from the concept that the RtI "process" is not "addressing the child's needs." Of course these are reasonable concerns from educators who want to know how much students are actually benefiting from their instruction or whether a biologically-based disability may be interfering with student learning. Scholars have continued to increase the number of weeks/data points needed to alter interventions and make recommendations because a strong indicator of how the student is performing in light of intervention must be obtained (Shapiro, 2013). Moreover, it generally takes at least 8 weeks for students to begin to show any response to intervention (Kilanowski, 2010a).

The upcoming video provides a brief oversight and explanation of why so many data points are needed prior to making an intervention change. It is important for teachers and administrators to remember that data collection in RtI is meant to inform their instruction and not simply guide practices towards a CSE referral. RtI is not a special education referral process but a general education initiative to prevent future learning delays. There is a clear need to alter our practices in data collection. The less data collection on a student, the more unreliable and invalid our practices are when making high stakes decisions regarding a student's movement throughout the tiers or into special education. In fact, we may be labeling children as disabled who simply need more time to respond to intervention given their age/grade or who simply need a switch in intervention.

"There is a clear need to alter our practices in data collection. The less data collection on a student, the more unreliable and invalid our practices are when making high-stakes decisions regarding a student's movement throughout the tiers or into special education."

"Christ et al., (2013) revealed that 12 – 14 weeks of data may provide educators with more valid and reliable data in the decision making process."

Grade Identified as Dyslexic	% Brought to Grade Level w/ Intervention
Grade 1 & 2	82%
Grade 3	46%
Grades 5 – 7	10 – 15%
Forman et al., 1996	Figure 9

The earlier evidence-based intervention takes place and progress monitoring occurs, the better chance students have at meeting grade-level expectations. Emphasis of implementing effective RtI/models should be placed at the grades K – 2 levels in order to have the best chance at remediating learning deficits and preventing future learning delays.

CLICK HERE TO PLAY COMMON CAVEATS
TO RtI IMPLEMENTATION VIDEO

STEPS TO DATA COLLECTION & RtI:

Step 1: Universal Screening:

- Universally screen all students using Curriculum-Based Measures such as DIBELS or AIMSweb (Do ***NOT*** use the SRI to universally screen all students for RtI).

Step 2: Determine Risk Using Cut Points:

What is a cut point?

- A cut point is a score on the scale of a screening tool or a progress monitoring tool. For universal screeners, educators use the cut point to determine whether to provide additional intervention.

For progress monitoring tools, educators use the cut point to determine whether the student has demonstrated adequate response, whether to make an instructional change, and whether to move the student to more or less intensive services" (Shinn, 2007). There is a growing research base that suggests that students with LD are typically performing below the 25th percentile on normed assessments such as DIBELS or AIMSweb (Shinn, 2007). Therefore, it is generally recommended that students who fall below the 25th percentile are in need of more intensive intervention at the Tier II level. Students who fall at or below the 10th percentile are at extreme risk.

Students who fall below the 25th percentile on DIBELS or AIMSweb CBM for their grade level should be identified for follow-up progress monitoring or entered into Tier II intervention services (National Center on Response to Intervention, 2010; Shinn, 2007). Students who fall at or below the 10th percentile are at extreme risk.

Step 3: Continued Progress Monitoring at Tier II Level:

A) *Small group intervention.* Students who enter Tier II intervention services should receive small group (3 – 6 students) push-in or pull-out instruction that is evidence-based through programs such as Road to the Code or Read Naturally. IEP students should not be in the small group as RtI is a general education initiative.

B) *Collect 12 – 14 CBM (DIBELS or AIMSweb) data points* should be collected on a bi-weekly basis before changing Tiers (Back to Tier 1 or to Tier III). Students who progress above 25th percentile on national norm CBM data can move to Tier 1.

**Takes at least 8 weeks of evidence-based reading instruction implemented with fidelity for students to show progress on CBM which is why 12 to 14 weeks of data or data points of DIBELS is suggested.

C) *Individual Goal Setting Using Rates of Improvement (ROI):*

Rate of Improvement: Typical rates of learning growth have been identified for large groups of students using certain measures (i.e. DIBELS does not publish their ROI which is why many districts and scholars prefer AIMSweb). Since, DIBELS does not publish their ROI's, we set a student's individual goal by cross-referencing AIMSweb's published ROI's.

Growth rates are calculated as the average weekly gain in a skill evidenced by students at a grade level (Kilanowski, 2011). For example a student's ROI or growth rate may be 0.9 words per week

Why is utilization of individualized ROI important?
- For students referred to Tier II, the national goal may be too ambitious for them to reach by the end of the year. Therefore, establishing individual goals and comparing the student's individual ROI to that of the national average is critical in determining if adequate progress is being made.

How to implement?

Using growth rate,

1) Multiply rate by number of weeks left until the aim date (date you expect student to reach goal-usually end of the year)

2) Add baseline score. *Can set goal for sooner than end of year though.

Spring Goal Calc DORF:

0.89 (ROI) x 23 (wks. left in year from 01/28/13) = 20.47 + 54 (Winter benchmark/baseline score) = 74.47

D) *Calculation of Rate of Growth Calculation or Individual ROI: STEPS*

1) Subtract lowest data pt. score from highest data pt. score

2) Divide difference between number of weeks (e.g. 10 weeks for 10 data points)

3) Use that number & multiply by Standard Deviation of 1.5.

E) *Calculate Individual. Rate of Improvement (ROI)*

On the following page, figure 10 provides an example of the steps in context.

NOTE:
- Users of DIBLES and AIMSweb should use regression rate of improvement when possible.

Example of Progress Monitoring Interpretation/Write-Up
Figure 10

ASSESSMENT RESULTS DORF:

DIBELS Oral Reading Fluency (DORF) is an individually administered Curriculum-Based Measure designed to assess the accuracy and fluency that a student can read connected text in one minute (DIBELS Oral Reading Fluency, n. d.). More specifically, DORF is a standardized set of passages designed to identify children who may need additional instructional support in reading and to monitor progress towards instructional goals (DIBELS Oral Reading Fluency, n. d.). Administration of DORF involves providing the student with a passage to read aloud for one minute. Words that are omitted, substituted, and hesitations of more than three seconds are scored as errors (DIBELS Oral Reading Fluency, n. d.). Words that are self-corrected within three seconds are scored as accurate with the number of correct words per minute for the passage being the oral reading fluency score (DIBELS Oral Reading Fluency, n. d.). The concept behind DORF is to assess whether a student is a fluent and accurate reader as those students whose decoding processes are automatic are better able to allocate their attention to the comprehension and meaning of the text (DIBELS Oral Reading Fluency, n. d.). DORF is first administered to children midway through their first grade year through the end of sixth grade.

S. D.'s DORF progress monitoring data and accompanying graph for the 2015 – 2016 school year are illustrated below. A third chart outlines DIBELS national benchmark goals and levels for the first three months of the second grade year. The fourth chart displays a comparable Oral Reading Fluency Curriculum-Based Measure from the Academic Improvement Measurement System or AIMSweb. The fourth chart has been included as DIBELS does not currently publish rates of improvement and thus individual progress monitoring goals cannot be calculated using DIBELS national data. However, individual progress monitoring goals can be calculated utilizing AIMSweb's published ROI's.

S. D.'s DIBELS Progress Monitoring Data: Oral Reading Fluency

Date	*09/12	09/19	09/26	10/02	10/09	10/16	10/23	10/30	11/07	11/14	11/21	11/28	12/04	12/11
Correct	2	0	1	1	1	2	2	3	3	3	4	3	5	5
Errors	4	6	5	5	6	8	8	8	10	13	13	12	11	14

*Fall Benchmark

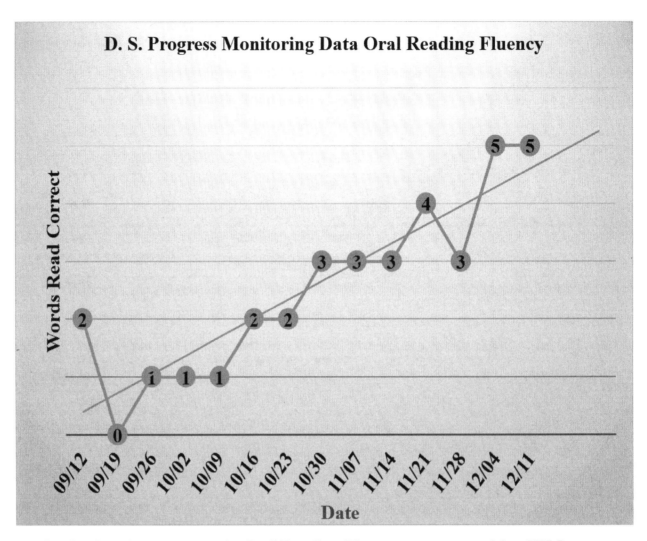

D. S. Progress Monitoring Data Oral Reading Fluency

Lack of student progress in Oral Reading Fluency as measured by CBM over a 14 week time period. <u>Users of DIBLES and AIMSweb should use regression rate of improvement when possible.</u>

**Recent studies and meta-analysis revealed 8 or less data points were unreliable and invalid in making recommendations for increasing intervention placement and special education referrals (Shapiro, 2013; Christ, 2013). Shapiro (2013) & Christ (2013) suggest that 12 – 14 weeks of data per Tier. *It typically takes a student 8 weeks of intervention to begin to show any significant improvement on a CBM.

National AIMSweb Benchmark (Second Grade) Fall: Oral Reading Fluency

Grade 2	%ile	Fall		Winter		Spring		ROI
		Num	WRC	Num	WRC	Num	WRC	----
Chart Area	90		115		140		156	1.14
	75		88		115		131	1.19
	50		62		88		106	1.22
	25		35		64		82	1.31
	10		17		39		59	1.17
	Mean		64		90		106	1.17
	Std Dev	38282	37	38282	38	38282	38	0.03
S. D.	*<10*		*10*		*--*		*S. D. Goal = 45.92*	*S. D. ROI = 0.54*

S. D. Spring Goal Calculation DORF:
- 1.22 (ROI) x 36 (weeks left in year) = 43.92 + 2 (fall benchmark score) = 45.92

* S. D. Individual. Rate of Improvement (ROI) Calculation:
- 5 – 0 = 5 ÷ 14 (highest - lowest data pt. ÷ # of data points.) = 0.357 x 1.5 = 0.54 (act. ROI)

Steps Broken Down for Individual Goal Calculation:

A) Goal Calculation

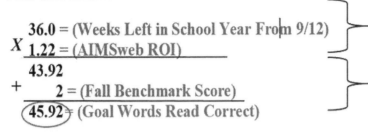

$$\begin{array}{l} 36.0 = \text{(Weeks Left in School Year From 9/12)} \\ X \ \underline{1.22 = \text{(AIMSweb ROI)}} \\ 43.92 \\ + \ \underline{2 = \text{(Fall Benchmark Score)}} \\ \boxed{45.92} = \text{(Goal Words Read Correct)} \end{array}$$

Step 1: Multiply weeks left in school year and Rate of Improvement. Use AIMSweb chart and 50th percentile highlighted in green

Step 2: Add benchmark or baseline score to calculate goal.

Goal = __45.92__ Words Read Correct

B) Rate of Improvement Calculation

1) *Subtract the highest date point from the lowest data point*

5	–	0	=	5
(Highest Data Pt)		(Lowest Data Pt.)		

2) *Divide your answer from Step 1 into the # of weeks/data points*

5 ÷ 14 = 0.357
(# of weeks/data points)

3) *Multiply your answer from step 2 by the standard deviation at the 50th percentile to obtain the words the child is gaining per week.*

0.357 x 1.5 = ⓪.54 (Gaining 0.54 words per week)
(SD)

4) *Compare student to average words per week students his/her age are making at the 50th percentile*

__0.54__ (Gaining 0.54 words per week; Avg. is 1.22 words per week = **minimal progress**

Sample Write-Up

End of the year write-up with DIBELS & Patterns of Strengths & Weaknesses:

Currently, S. D. reads 5 words correct per minute with 14 errors from DIBELS second grade Oral Reading Fluency CBM. S. D.'s Oral Reading Fluency score of 5 words read correct (WRC) indicates that he continues to be in the At-Risk range when compared to his same-age peers. According to national ORF AIMSweb data, S. D. is below the 10th percentile and in the Well-Below Average range. Upcoming winter AIMSWEB benchmark data indicates that at the 50th percentile, second grade students are expected to read at least 88 WRC.

Examination of S. D.'s weekly rate of improvement (ROI = 0.54 WPM) reveals that he is not meeting expected weekly progress (ROI = 1.22 WRC) to obtain his end of the year goal of 45.92 WRC. S. D.'s current weekly rate of improvement of 0.54 WRC displays that he is making less progress than second grade students at the 50th percentile (1.22 WRC). His current ratio of deficiency is 2.3 words read correct, indicating that he is progressing 2.3 words lower than expected. S. D.'s ratio of deficiency on DORF is greater than 2.0 and displays a significant lack of progress in reading fluency. These results may be suggestive of a student with a severe learning deficit in reading fluency which may impact his reading comprehension.

Evaluation of S. D's *Patterns of Strengths and Weaknesses* further bolster significant reading deficits. His recent state English test score fell in the Well-Below Proficient range with a score of 600. In order to reach proficiency, he needed a score of 700. Additionally, S. D.'s grades in reading fell at the unsatisfactory level with a D on his least reading test on tricky. Finally, S. D's SRI Reading score of 250 indicates that he remains an emergent reader. In order to reach proficiency, S. D. needs a score between 300 to 600. S. D.'s scores indicate that he continues to need intensive intervention in the areas of reading fluency and comprehension to remediate deficits in the aforementioned areas despite Tier III services being implemented for 14 weeks. S. D.'s continued deficits in reading may warrant a psycho-educational evaluation to determine whether he needs special education support to address his unique learning needs in reading fluency and reading comprehension.

User-Friendly Template for Struggling Reader

Currently, _____ (Student Name) reads ____ words correct per minute with ____ errors from DIBELS second grade Oral Reading Fluency CBM. _____ (Student Name) Oral Reading Fluency score of 5 words read correct (WRC) indicates that he continues to be in the At-Risk range when compared to his same-age peers. According to national ORF AIMSweb data, _____ (Student Name) is at the ____ percentile and in the _____ range. Upcoming winter AIMSWEB benchmark data indicates that at the 50th percentile, _____ grade students are expected to read at least 88 WRC.

Examination of _____'s (Student Name) weekly rate of improvement (ROI = ____ WPM) reveals that he/she is not meeting expected weekly progress (ROI = ____ WRC) to obtain his end of the year goal of 45.92 WRC. _____ (Student Name) current weekly rate of improvement of 0.54 WRC displays that he/she is making less progress than ____ grade students at the 50th percentile (____ WRC). These results may be suggestive of a student with a severe learning deficit in reading fluency which may impact reading comprehension.

Evaluation of _____'s (Student Name) *Academic Patterns of Strengths and Weaknesses* further bolster significant reading deficits. _____'s (Student Name) recent state English test score fell in the Well-Below Proficient range with a score of _____. In order to reach proficiency, he/she needed a score of 700. Additionally, _____ (Student Name) grades in reading fell at the _____ level with a ____ on his/her least reading test. Finally, _____ (Student Name) SRI Reading score of _____ indicates that he/she remains an emergent reader. In order to reach proficiency, _____ (Student Name) needs a score between ____ to ____. _____'s (Student Name) scores indicate that he continues to need intensive intervention in the areas of reading fluency and comprehension to remediate deficits in the aforementioned areas despite Tier III services being implemented for 14 weeks. _____'s (Student Name) continued deficits in reading may warrant a psycho-educational evaluation to determine whether he/she needs special education support to address his/her unique learning needs in reading fluency and reading comprehension.

(Kilanowski, 2010; Schaffer, 2016)

Articles & Interventions for RtI

#'s Correspond to Resource links on following Page

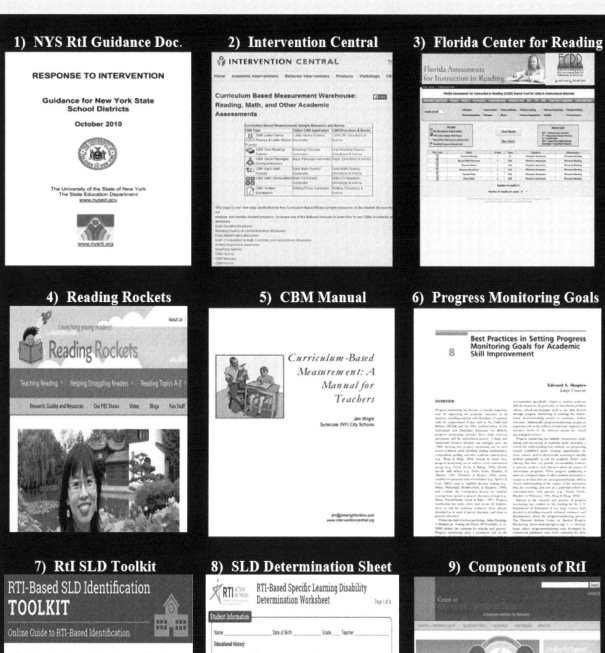

1) NYS RtI Guidance Doc.

2) Intervention Central

3) Florida Center for Reading

4) Reading Rockets

5) CBM Manual

6) Progress Monitoring Goals

7) RtI SLD Toolkit

8) SLD Determination Sheet

9) Components of RtI

School-Wide Positive Behavior Support

What is SWPBS?

School-Wide Positive Behavior Support (SWPBS) is a three-tiered early intervention service delivery model that establishes positive behavioral supports to help students achieve academic and social success (Frey, Lingo, & Nelson, 2010). SWPBS is a proactive model that promotes a positive and welcoming school environment by clearly outlining and teaching behavioral expectations, rewarding pro-social behavior, improving student supervision, and screening/progress monitoring students to identify and track behavioral concerns (Sprick & Bogmeirer, 2010). SWPBS is preventative in that it attempts to identify and remediate behavior problems before they occur. Through SWPBS student behavior and social support increases in intensity and duration depending on whether the student responds to the behavior interventions provided (Sprick & Bogmeirer, 2010). SWPBS contrasts the reactionary and exclusionary model of managing student behavior by attempting to avoid corporal punishment, suspension, or expulsion of students (Sprick & Bogmeirer, 2010). According to Sprick and Bogmeirer (2010) and the Council on School Health (2013), reactionary and exclusionary approaches to student discipline increase risk for alienating students, cause emotional harm, elevate school drop-out rates, and foster an uncaring and cold school environment.

SWPBS maximizes academic engagement and achievement for all students by:

- Reducing disciplinary referrals, suspensions and expulsions while increasing academic performance.

- Increasing the consistent use of positive teaching and reinforcement strategies for behavior

- Using more engaging, responsive, preventive and productive approaches to problematic behavior

- Improving supports for students whose behaviors require more specialized assistance (e.g., emotional and behavioral disorders, mental health) (What is PBIS?, n. d., para. 5)

Tier 1

At the Tier 1 level of SWPBS, primary prevention practices are implemented and apply to all students to foster a school environment that is safe and nurturing. Thus, Tier 1 includes "all the system level work that is done as part of a school's PBS efforts to improve safety, climate, discipline, motivation, and school connectedness" (Sprick & Bogmeirer, 2010, p. 439). Examples of Tier 1 practices include defining and teaching behavioral expectations for all students, applying positive consequences to promote desired behavior, modifying environmental arrangements, and providing active supervision (Frey, Lingo, & Nelson, 2010). Moreover, Tier 1 of SWPBS involves universal screening of all students to identify those who are not responding to Tier 1 intervention. Of note is that 80 percent of students should not need Tier 2 and Tier 3 interventions.

Tier 2

Tier 2 targets students who are not responding to Tier 1 interventions (Sprick & Borgmeier, 2010). Thus, students at Tier 2 are at-risk for "developing patterns of severe problem behavior for a variety of reasons, including poor peer relations, low academic achievement, or chaotic home environments" (Frey et al., 2010 p. 411). Overall, Tier 2 interventions attempt to prevent recurrent academic failure and problem behavior. Therefore, Tier 2 interventions focus on instruction on targeted skills, self-monitoring, frequent performance feedback concerning target behaviors, and peer tutoring (Frey et al., 2010). Generally, Tier 2 interventions should produce rapid improvements in students' behavior and be easy to implement (Frey et al., 2010). Examples of Tier 2 interventions include Social Academic Instructional Groups, mentoring programs, check-in/check-out systems (figure 12), and behavior contracts (Frey et al., 2010). Students should be progress monitored to assess their responsiveness to these interventions through their school attendance, office referrals, suspensions, or expulsions. Of note is that approximately, 15 to 20 percent of student may need Tier 2 supports.

Tier 3

Finally, Tier 3 focuses on students who have not responded to Tier 1 and Tier 2 interventions. Therefore, these students have chronic and severe behavioral or emotional difficulties that require intensive and individualized supports. These intensive and individualized supports require greater amounts of time, expertise, and resources to be effectively implemented with teams being devised for each individual student (Frey et al., 2010). These teams typically consist of general educators, special educators, administrators, school psychologists, mental health professionals, support service personnel, and the child's parents (Frey et al., 2010).

Through the development of these teams, a behavioral intervention plan (BIP) is developed for the student to address specific areas of concern. Furthermore, wraparound services may be implemented as school based supports may not meet all the particular needs of a student at this level. Thus, students at Tier 3 may receive additional support outside the school from medical, mental health, and community service providers (Sprick & Borgmeier, 2010). Finally, school psychologists may be utilized at the Tier 3 level to provide students with clinical-based counseling in the school setting. At Tier 3 ongoing data collection is used to monitor the student's response to the BIP and wraparound services. Approximately 1 to 5 percent of students will not respond to Tier 2 interventions and require Tier 3 support.

CLICK HERE TO PLAY PBIS VIDEO

What can I use for screening or progress monitoring in SWPBS?

Universal screening and progress monitoring tools for assessing student behavior are relatively new. However, a growing number of screeners and progress monitoring tools exist and some are even available for free online. A description of some of the most commonly used screeners and progress monitoring tools can be found below.

School-Wide Information System (SWIS)
Data and Office Referral management system

- Perhaps, the most widely used tool for identifying students with externalizing behavior is the School-wide Information System or SWIS. According to the New York PBIS Technical Assistance Center, SWIS is a "web-based information system designed to help school personnel to use office referral data to design school and individual student interventions (What is PBIS?, n.d., para 1)." SWIS is based off of three components: an efficient system for gathering information, an internet-based computer application for data entry and generation of reports, and a process for using school, grade level, and

44

individual student data for decision making (What is PBIS?, n.d.). For more information on SWIS, visit: https://www.PBISApps.org.

Student Risk Screening Scale (SRSS)
1 – 2 minute Universal Screener (use up to 3 times per year)
SSRS Available for Free CLICK HERE

- The Student Risk Screening Scale is a brief, valid, and reliable universal screener used to identify student risk and presence of displaying problem behaviors (Drummond, 1993; Walker, 2009). The SRSS utilizes a Likert rating scale to compare each student in the class across seven behavioral criteria (i.e. lies, cheats, sneaks, steals, behavior problems, peer rejections, low achievement, negative attitude, and aggressive behavior) to determine students who are at-risk for displaying anti-social behaviors (Drummond, 1993; Walker, 2009). The SRSS can be administered three times per year for youth at the K – 12 grade levels (Walker, 2009). Further information and directions on how to use the SRSS can be found by clicking the link here. Total scores on the SRSS range from 0 to 21. Scores from 0 to 3 indicate low-risk status. Scores from 4 to 7 indicate moderate risk and scores from 8 to 21 indicate high risk for behavioral concern.

Strengths & Differences Questionnaire
5 minute Universal Screener (Use up to 3 times per year)
Strengths & Differences Questionnaire Available for Free CLICK HERE

- The Strengths and Differences Questionnaire is a brief behavioral universal screening questionnaire that consists of 25 items. The SDQ assesses 3 to 16 year old students across 5 scales of which include 1) emotional symptoms 2) conduct problems 3) hyperactivity/inattention 4) peer relationship problems and 5) prosocial behavior (What is the SDQ?, n. d.)._ The same 25 questions that are provided for teachers to complete are also given to parents. Finally, a self-report version is available for youth ages 11 – 16. The SDQ is available for free and is published in a wide-variety of languages on the publisher's website (What is the SDQ?, n. d.).

Systematic Screening for Behavior Disorders (SSBD)
Universal Screener

- The Systematic Screening for Behavior Disorders (SSBD) is an evidence-based screener for identifying children who may be at risk for developing internalizing and externalizing behavior disorders (SSBD Online, n. d.). The SSBD utilizes increasingly precise screening instruments to identify youth who are at-risk for developing behavioral disorders (Saeki et al., 2011). The three measures involved in the SSBD screening process include teacher nominations, ratings, and observations (Saeki et al., 2011).

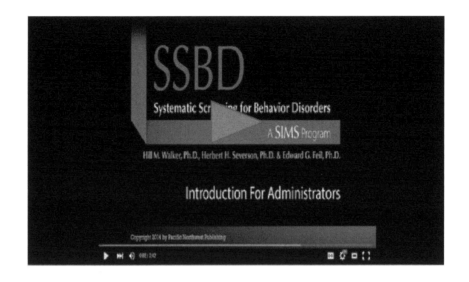

CLICK HERE TO PLAY SYSTEMATIC SCREENING FOR BEHAVIOR DISORDERS VIDEO

Graphing Tools, Behavior, and Classroom Management Tools/Links

1. *SUNY OSWEGO: Graphing Made Easy*

2. *Intervention Central Chartdog*

3. *Class Dojo*

4. *PBISWorld Data Tracking*

5. *Create a Graph*

Figure 11

Behavior SWPBS Flow Chart

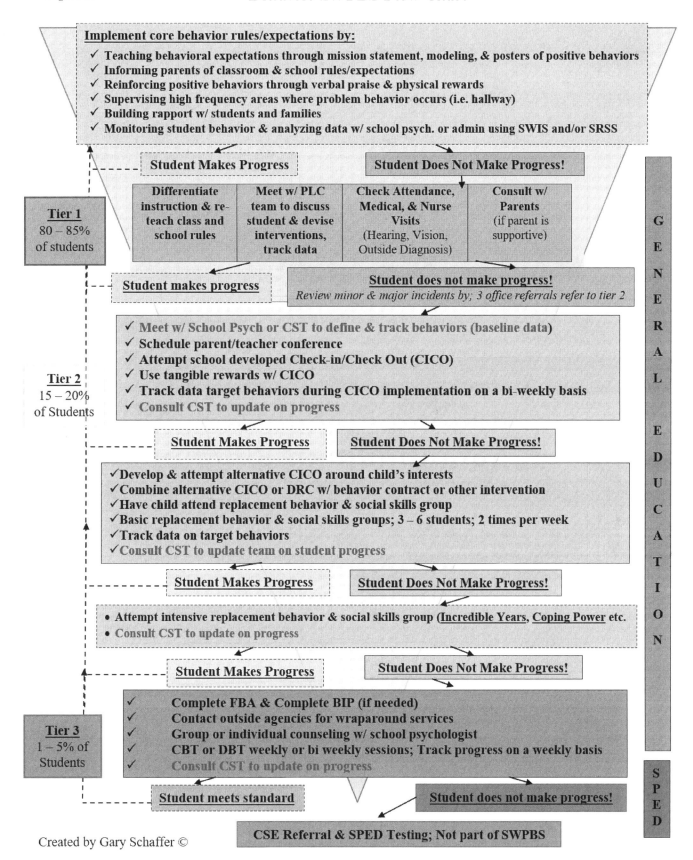

Implement core behavior rules/expectations by:
- ✓ Teaching behavioral expectations through mission statement, modeling, & posters of positive behaviors
- ✓ Informing parents of classroom & school rules/expectations
- ✓ Reinforcing positive behaviors through verbal praise & physical rewards
- ✓ Supervising high frequency areas where problem behavior occurs (i.e. hallway)
- ✓ Building rapport w/ students and families
- ✓ Monitoring student behavior & analyzing data w/ school psych. or admin using SWIS and/or SRSS

Student Makes Progress | **Student Does Not Make Progress!**

Tier 1
80 – 85% of students

| Differentiate instruction & re-teach class and school rules | Meet w/ PLC team to discuss student & devise interventions, track data | Check Attendance, Medical, & Nurse Visits (Hearing, Vision, Outside Diagnosis) | Consult w/ Parents (if parent is supportive) |

Student makes progress

Student does not make progress!
Review minor & major incidents by; 3 office referrals refer to tier 2

- ✓ Meet w/ School Psych or CST to define & track behaviors (baseline data)
- ✓ Schedule parent/teacher conference
- ✓ Attempt school developed Check-in/Check Out (CICO)
- ✓ Use tangible rewards w/ CICO
- ✓ Track data target behaviors during CICO implementation on a bi-weekly basis
- ✓ Consult CST to update on progress

Tier 2
15 – 20% of Students

Student Makes Progress | **Student Does Not Make Progress!**

- ✓ Develop & attempt alternative CICO around child's interests
- ✓ Combine alternative CICO or DRC w/ behavior contract or other intervention
- ✓ Have child attend replacement behavior & social skills group
- ✓ Basic replacement behavior & social skills groups; 3 – 6 students; 2 times per week
- ✓ Track data on target behaviors
- ✓ Consult CST to update team on student progress

Student Makes Progress | **Student Does Not Make Progress!**

- • Attempt intensive replacement behavior & social skills group (**Incredible Years**, **Coping Power** etc.
- • Consult CST to update on progress

Student Makes Progress | **Student Does Not Make Progress!**

Tier 3
1 – 5% of Students

- ✓ Complete FBA & Complete BIP (if needed)
- ✓ Contact outside agencies for wraparound services
- ✓ Group or individual counseling w/ school psychologist
- ✓ CBT or DBT weekly or bi weekly sessions; Track progress on a weekly basis
- ✓ Consult CST to update on progress

Student meets standard | **Student does not make progress!**

CSE Referral & SPED Testing; Not part of SWPBS

GENERAL EDUCATION

SPED

Created by Gary Schaffer ©

Sample Check-in/Check-Out 1

Figure 12

Student Name: Date:					3 = Excellent 2 = Good 1 = I know I could do better						
Period/Subject	**Safe**			**Responsible**			**Respectful**			**Teacher Comments**		
	3	2	1	3	2	1	3	2	1			
	3	2	1	3	2	1	3	2	1			
	3	2	1	3	2	1	3	2	1			
	3	2	1	3	2	1	3	2	1			
	3	2	1	3	2	1	3	2	1			
	3	2	1	3	2	1	3	2	1			
	3	2	1	3	2	1	3	2	1			
	3	2	1	3	2	1	3	2	1			
	3	2	1	3	2	1	3	2	1			

Total Possible Points: 72. My total points earned for the day was _____. I need _____ out of 72 points to earn my reward.

Additional space for teacher comments:

_____

_____

Parent Signature: _____   **Date:** _____

Check-In/Check-Out (CICO) Instructions

Directions: Generally keep Check-In/Check-Out's short, simple, *consistent* and positive across all settings using the following format. Feedback should not exceed two minutes.

Step 1 A: (If child met w/ you in the morning)

Say a variation of:

- "Hey (child's name), it's good to see you today. Let's see how you did in this (morning, afternoon)."

Say a variation of:

Step 1 B: (If this is the child's first Check-In for today say)

- "Good morning (child's name). I am glad you are here today. Let's go over our goals for today." (Refer to child's behavior contract or goals you discussed prior to CICO going into place. i.e. safe hands and feet, working hard). "Remember, if you meet your goals, you will get a BIG reward this afternoon!"

Step 2 A: (If child met goals)

Say variation of:

- *"Hey (child's name). Let's see how you are doing! Wow!!!! Look at how many points you have and you did great last period too!! Keep it up!! Remember for this class I want you to keep following our school/classroom rules of _____ and _____." **Here is your reward."***

- *"Remember for this class I want you to keep following our school/classroom rules of _____ and _____ you earn another reward."*

Step 2 B: (If child did not meet goals)

Say variation of:

- *"Hey (child's name). Let's see how you are doing! Oh no, I know you can earn more points than that. Hey, how about starting with my class you start earning those points by following the class/school rules of _____ and _____ so you can earn your reward. I know you can do it (child's name). Remember, you can still earn your prize. (If end of day, you can say well hey we all have our off days. How about tomorrow you come in and follow the school/classroom rules of _____ and _____ to earn your reward! I know you can do it!!!!"*

Figure 13

Sample Check-in/Check-Out 2

Student Name: _____

☺ = Excellent   😐 = Good   ☹ = I know I can do Better

Period/Subject	Peaceful			Responsible			Respectful			Teacher Comments
	☺	😐	☹	☺	😐	☹	☺	😐	☹	
	☺	😐	☹	☺	😐	☹	☺	😐	☹	
	☺	😐	☹	☺	😐	☹	☺	😐	☹	
	☺	😐	☹	☺	😐	☹	☺	😐	☹	
	☺	😐	☹	☺	😐	☹	☺	😐	☹	
	☺	😐	☹	☺	😐	☹	☺	😐	☹	
	☺	😐	☹	☺	😐	☹	☺	😐	☹	
	☺	😐	☹	☺	😐	☹	☺	😐	☹	

Additional space for teacher comments:

_____

_____

Parent Signature: _____   **Teacher Signature:** _____

Check-In/Check-Out (CICO) Instructions

Directions: Generally keep Check-In/Check-Out's short, simple, *consistent* and positive across all settings using the following format. Feedback should not exceed two minutes.

Step 1 A: (If child met w/ you in the morning)

Say a variation of:

- "Hey (child's name), it's good to see you today. Let's see how you did in this (morning, afternoon)."

Say a variation of:

Step 1 B: (If this is the child's first Check-In for today say)

- "Good morning (child's name). I am glad you are here today. Let's go over our goals for today." (Refer to child's behavior contract or goals you discussed prior to CICO going into place. i.e. safe hands and feet, working hard). "Remember, if you meet your goals, you will get a BIG reward this afternoon!"

Step 2 A: (If child met goals)

Say variation of:

- *"Hey (child's name). Let's see how you are doing! Wow!!!! Look at how many points you have and you did great last period too!! Keep it up!! Remember for this class I want you to keep following our school/classroom rules of _____ and _____."* **Here is your reward."**

- *"Remember for this class I want you to keep following our school/classroom rules of _____ and _____ you earn another reward."*

Step 2 B: (If child did not meet goals)

Say variation of:

- *"Hey (child's name). Let's see how you are doing! Oh no, I know you can earn more points than that. Hey, how about starting with my class you start earning those points by following the class/school rules of _____ and _____ so you can earn your reward. I know you can do it (child's name). Remember, you can still earn your prize. (If end of day, you can say well hey we all have our off days. How about tomorrow you come in and follow the school/classroom rules of _____ and _____ to earn your reward! I know you can do it!!!!"*

Figure 14

Sample Alternative Check-In/Check-Out

Name: _____

Date: _____

Directions: *Coco and his friends like dog bones and need your help. By making good choices and meeting your goal, you will help Coco and his friends get their dog bones. For your help, Coco will give you a REWARD!!!*

Coco

TIME OF CHECK-IN: _____

I NEED TO COLOR ____ OUT OF ____ OF COCO'S FRIENDS TO GET MY REWARD!

TIME OF CHECK-IN: _____

I NEED TO COLOR ____ OUT OF ____ OF COCO'S FRIENDS TO GET MY REWARD!

TIME OF CHECK-IN: _____

I NEED TO COLOR ____ OUT OF ____ OF COCO'S FRIENDS TO GET MY REWARD!

Total Points for day ____ out of ___

Check-In/Check-Out (CICO) Instructions

Directions: Generally keep Check-In/Check-Out's short, simple, *consistent* and positive across all settings using the following format. Feedback should not exceed two minutes.

Step 1 A: (If child met w/ you in the morning)

Say a variation of:

- "Hey (child's name), it's good to see you today. Let's see how you did in this (morning, afternoon)."

Say a variation of:

Step 1 B: (If this is the child's first Check-In for today say)

- "Good morning (child's name). I am glad you are here today. Let's go over our goals for today." (Refer to child's behavior contract or goals you discussed prior to CICO going into place. i.e. safe hands and feet, working hard). "Remember, if you meet your goals, you will get a BIG reward this afternoon!"

Step 2 A: (If child met goals)

Say variation of:

- "Hey (child's name). Let's see how you are doing! Wow!!!! Look at how many points you have and you did great last period too!! Keep it up!! Remember for this class I want you to keep following our school/classroom rules of _____ and _____." **Here is your reward."**

- "Remember for this class I want you to keep following our school/classroom rules of _____ and _____ you earn another reward."

Step 2 B: (If child did not meet goals)

Say variation of:

- "Hey (child's name). Let's see how you are doing! Oh no, I know you can earn more points than that. Hey, how about starting with my class you start earning those points by following the class/school rules of _____ and _____ so you can earn your reward. I know you can do it (child's name). Remember, you can still earn your prize. (If end of day, you can say well hey we all have our off days. How about tomorrow you come in and follow the school/classroom rules of _____ and _____ to earn your reward! I know you can do it!!!!"

SWPBS Interventions & Resources

#'s correspond to links of Resources on the Following Page

1) PBIS World

2) NYS PBIS Assistance Center

3) PBIS Description

4) Teacher Tools PBIS

5) NASP PBIS

6) SUNY Oswego Graphing

7) Student Risk Screening Scale

8) SWPBIS

9) Blueprint for SWPBIS

Social-Emotional Multi-Tiered Support

How Many Children Are In Need of Mental Health Services?

According to the National Alliance on Mental Illness (n. d.) and National Association of School Psychologists (2015), approximately 1 out of every 5 children suffer from a diagnosable mental health disorder severe enough to impede their daily life functioning and about 80% of children do not receive appropriate treatment for their condition. Of those children who do receive assistance, the majority (70 – 80%) receive mental health services in school (National Association of School Psychologists, 2015). In fact, students were found to be 21 times more likely to visit school-based centers for mental health concerns over community-based centers (Jusczak, Melinkovich, & Kaplan, 2003). With children receiving the vast majority of their mental health services in school, school psychologists are uniquely positioned to facilitate the development, delivery, and progress monitoring of mental and behavioral health services (National Association of School psychologists, 2015).

It has long been documented that students experiencing emotional and behavioral difficulties are underserved or unserved by the mental health and educational systems across the United States (Gresham, 2005). In NYS alone, 40 of 62 counties (65%) are designated as mental health shortage areas and approximately 3,111,401 people in the state reside in such areas (New York State Office of Mental Health, 2014). According to the New York State Education Department Office of Professions (2017), 35 counties have 20 or fewer licensed psychologists. Of the licensed psychologists in practice, it is largely unknown how many specialize in the diagnosis and treatment of childhood mental health disorders. Unfortunately, similar shortages of qualified mental health practitioners specializing in children exists throughout the United States (Gresham, 2005; National Alliance on Mental Illness, n. d.; National Association of School Psychologists, 2015). Through accessing school psychologists' unique skillset in mental health and education, schools may place children facing emotional and behavioral challenges in the best position for succeeding in and outside of the educational setting. For students in need of more intensive social, emotional, or behavioral services, school psychologists can help facilitate and coordinate a wraparound system of care that utilizes school and community-based services (National Association of School Psychologists, 2015).

Licensed Psychologists Per County in NYS

County	Number	County	Number	County	Number
Albany	238	Jefferson	22	Saratoga	100
Allegany	14	Kings	941	Schenectady	55
Bronx	216	Lewis	2	Schoharie	2
Broome	75	Livingston	11	Schuyler	6
Cattaraugus	10	Madison	17	Seneca	1
Cayuga	4	Monroe	339	Steuben	23
Chautauqua	7	Montgomery	5	St. Lawrence	17
Chemung	14	Nassau	1,247	Suffolk	879
Chenango	5	New York	3,395	Sullivan	17
Clinton	10	Niagara	19	Tioga	8
Columbia	24	Oneida	45	Tompkins	68
Cortland	11	Onondaga	209	Ulster	113
Delaware	8	Ontario	29	Warren	31
Dutchess	162	Orange	103	Washington	5
Erie	303	Orleans	3	Wayne	6
Essex	13	Oswego	10	Westchester	1,224
Franklin	10	Otsego	17	Wyoming	1
Fulton	11	Putnam	51	Yates	4
Genesee	5	Queens	555	**NYS TOTAL**	**11,118**
Greene	10	Rensselaer	36	**OTHER US**	**2,620**
Hamilton	2	Richmond	136	**NON-US**	**72**
Herkimer	2	Rockland	212	**TOTAL**	**13,810**

(NYS Office of Professions, 2017)

What is Emotional Disturbance?

Although 1 out of 5 children suffer from a diagnosable mental health condition, only a subset of these children will qualify for special education services as a student with Emotional Disturbance. According to Tibbets (2013), Emotional Disturbance is deliberately focused on that narrow range of students who have an identifiable emotional impairment that adversely affects their educational performance.

The Individuals with Disabilities Education Act (2004), defines Emotional Disturbance as a condition exhibiting one or more of the following characteristics over a long period of time and to a marked degree that adversely affects a child's educational performance:

i.   An inability to learn that cannot be explained by intellectual, sensory, or health factors.

ii. An inability to build or maintain satisfactory interpersonal relationships with peers and teachers.

iii. Inappropriate types of behavior or feelings under normal circumstances.

iv. A general pervasive mood of unhappiness or depression.

v.   A tendency to develop physical symptoms or fears associated with personal or school problems

vi. Emotional disturbance includes schizophrenia. The term does not apply to children who are socially maladjusted, unless it is determined that they have an emotional disturbance

What is Emotional Disturbance vs an Emotional Condition?

An analysis of Emotional Disturbance as defined by IDEA reveals that the definition describes a set of "limiting," yet often convoluted criteria, for defining ED. From the criteria, children who display emotional disturbance must exhibit an inability to learn, build or maintain satisfactory interpersonal relationships, experience inappropriate types or feelings under normal circumstances, have a general pervasive mood of unhappiness or depression, or display a tendency to develop symptoms or fears associated with personal or school problems long period of time and to a marked degree that adversely affects the child's educational performance.

Conversely, an emotional condition is short in duration, displayed relatively infrequently, may occur in certain circumstances or settings (i.e. in certain classes or in front of certain individuals), and may not adversely impact the child's overall educational performance over a long period of time. For example, a child who cries after losing a loved one does not automatically qualify as a student with an emotional disturbance unless the child's condition lasts for an extended period of time and is severe enough that it directly impacts their educational performance. Therefore, students who may be easily identifiable by outside clinicians as having an emotional condition (i.e. anxiety, depression) are often found ineligible for special education services because of the lack of significant impact of their disorder on their educational performance (Tibbets, 2013). A further analysis of the characteristics of emotional disturbance can be found in the following chart based on Tibbets (2013) and Gresham (2005) examination of ED criteria.

ED Criteria	Description
Over a Long Period of Time To be classified as emotionally disturbed, an emotional condition must occur *over a long period of time* as opposed to being a temporary decrease in emotional functioning/well-being. **Over a Long Period of Time** = *Duration*	**ED Should be Present 6 Months or Longer.** To be considered as having emotional disturbance, a child must display a decrease in emotional functioning and well-being that has occurred for an extended period of time. A 6- month-time-frame both reflects DSM-V and congress' period to distinguish between expected resolutions to identifiable stressor(s) (i.e. loss of a loved one) and temporary transitory difficulties (Tibbets, 2013). This time period also allows for school staff to attempt emotional and behavioral interventions (Tibbets, 2013).
To a Marked Degree An emotional condition must be displayed to a "marked degree." To a marked degree suggests the severity of an emotional condition as defined by the pervasiveness and intensity of the condition (Gresham, 2005). **To a Marked Degree** = *Severity*	**Pervasiveness and Intensity** *Pervasiveness* – An emotional condition should occur across multiple settings in order for a child to qualify as a student with Emotional Disturbance (Gresham, 2005; Tibbets, 2013). For example, a child with emotional disturbance may display episodes across their school day and at home as opposed to only crying in math class. *Intensity* – The severity in which the emotional condition impacts academic achievement, interpersonal relations, and social skills both in the home and school environments.
Adversely Affects Educational Performance To be classified with an ED, a child must display an Emotional Condition in the school setting that significantly impedes his/her child's to benefit from instruction & supports in the general education setting. **Adversely Affects Ed. Performance** = *Impact on Ed. Performance*	**Current Edu. Placement Doesn't Meet Needs** Despite interventions, the emotional condition adversely affects the child's performance in the general education setting. Classification & placement in a different educational setting is needed to meet the student's needs & help them succeed academically (Tibbets, 2013).

What is Emotional Disturbance vs. Social Maladjustment?

One of the most controversial caveats of the emotional disturbance definition is the "social maladjustment" exclusionary clause. IDEA (2004) indicates that emotional disturbance: *"includes schizophrenia. The term does not apply to children who are <u>socially maladjusted</u>, unless it is determined that they have an emotional disturbance."* In other words, students who are socially maladjusted can only qualify for special education services if it is found that they also have an emotional disturbance. A student who is only found socially maladjusted would not qualify for special education services (Gresham, 2005).

To date, social maladjustment has never been defined in federal law and no universal definition has been adopted (Gresham, 2005; Merrell & Walker, 2004). Still, educators and legislators have generally "assumed" social maladjustment is defined by anti-social, acting-out, and delinquent behaviors that tend to be external, purposeful, harmful, and undercontrolled in nature (Merrell & Walker, 2004; Tibbets, 2013). Examples of impairments that best exemplify social maladjustment include Conduct and Oppositional Defiant Disorder. Conversely, emotional disturbance tends to be thought of as disorders that are internal, purposeless and overcontrolled in nature such as depression, anxiety, PTSD, and social phobia (Merrell & Walker, 2004; Tibbets, 2013).

Historically schools have excluded socially maladjusted students from receiving special education services based on the premise that these students demonstrate problems in conduct in which they are in control of and responsible for. Under IDEA, students who are viewed as "in control" of their delinquent behavior(s) do not have a legitimate educational disability in need of special education services (Gresham, 2005). Therefore, inclusion of the social maladjustment clause within the ED definition has long been cited as a means to "satisfy the concerns of legislators and educational administrators who did not want schools to be mandated to provide services to delinquent and antisocial youth." (Merrell & Walter, 2004, p. 901). Federal policy makers believed that by including the social maladjustment clause into the definition for emotional disturbance the result would be a special education category that was not too broad or costly to districts (Tibbets, 2013).

Interestingly, the federal definition of ED adopted by congress in 1975 was based on Eli Bower's 1957 protocol for identifying students in need of severe emotional and behavioral difficulties (Merrell & Walker, 2004; Tibbets, 2013). In Bower's original definition of ED, he did not include a social maladjustment clause. Additionally, many scholars do not support the inclusion of social maladjustment in the federal definition for ED, believing that emotionally disturbed and socially maladjusted students are not separate entities (Gresham, 2005; Merrell & Walker, 2003; Tibbets, 2013). Overall, the federal definition for ED has been cited as vague and convoluted causing much confusion among educators. For example, mental health practitioners tend to consider behaviors that are internal in nature (depression, anxiety) as the most powerful predictors for ED, while educators tend to cite externalizing behaviors (i.e. defiance, challenging authority) as the most prominent factors for identifying ED (Merrell & Walker, 2004; Tibbets, 2013). Figure 16 compares emotional disturbance and social maladjustment.

Comparison of Emotional Disturbance and Social Maladjustment

Emotional Disturbance (ED)	Social Maladjustment (SM) Traditional Views of Social Maladjustment
• Not a medical diagnosis under the Diagnostic and Statistical Manual of Mental Disorders.	• Not a medical diagnosis under the Diagnostic and Statistical Manual of Mental Disorders.
• Is an educational classification for providing students special education services/qualifies for special education services	• Is not an educational classification for providing students special education services/does not qualify for special education services
• Student is suspected to meet or meets DSM criteria for depression, dysthymia, bi-polar disorder, anxiety disorders	• Student is suspected to meet or meets DSM criteria for Conduct Disorder or Oppositional Defiant Disorder
• Internal and purposeless behaviors that are thought to be out of the students control and are viewed as skill deficits. Examples of such behaviors include social isolation, constant crying, anxiety, somatic complaints, and unfounded fears	• Anti-social, acting-out, and delinquent behaviors that tend to be external, purposeful, harmful, and within the student's control. Examples of such behaviors include aggression, disruption, lying, defiance, and stealing
• Engages in behaviors as an emotional release or to avoid sources of angst (crying, angry outbursts, social withdrawal, missing school). Behaviors are not to maintain a social status within a deviant or socio-cultural peer group	• Student engages in antisocial and delinquent behavior to maintain a status within a deviant or socio-cultural peer group

Adapted from Merrell & Walker, 2004; Tibbets, 2013; Wayne County Regional Educational Services Agency, 2004

**To date, social maladjustment has never been defined in federal law and no universal definition has been adopted (Gresham, 2005; Merrell & Walker, 2004). Generally, many scholars are non-supportive of the social maladjustment exclusionary clause in the definition of emotional disturbance (Gresham, 2005; Merrell & Walker, 2004; Tibbets, 2013).

Comparison of Emotional Disturbance and Social Maladjustment

Emotional Disturbance (ED)	Social Maladjustment (SM) Traditional Views of Social Maladjustment
Figure 16	
• Difficulty making friends; ignored or rejected. Tends to be a loner	• Accepted by a same delinquent or socio-cultural subgroup
• Perceived as bizarre, strange, fearful, or anxious; often made fun of	• Perceived as cool, tough, relaxed
• School is a source of confusion or angst; does much better w/ structure	• Dislikes school, except as a social outlet; rebels against rules and structure
• Poor self-concept, overly dependent, anxious, fearful, distorts reality, mood swings	• Inflated self-concept, independent, underdeveloped conscience, blames others, excessive bravado
• Unable to comply with teacher or staff requests; has difficulty asking for help or is needy	• Unwilling to comply with teacher or staff requests and rejects help
• Remorseful, self-critical, may blame self	• Remorseless, blames others
• Is aggressive due to internalizing disorder; may want to hurt self to escape pain	• Hurts others to obtain what he/she wants

Adapted from Merrell & Walker, 2004; Tibbets, 2013; Wayne County Regional Educational Services Agency, 2004

**To date, social maladjustment has never been defined in federal law and no universal definition has been adopted (Gresham, 2005; Merrell & Walker, 2004). Generally, many scholars are non-supportive of the social maladjustment exclusionary clause in the definition of emotional disturbance (Gresham, 2005; Merrell & Walker, 2004; Tibbets, 2013).

What is the Prevalence of Emotional Disturbance?

The United States Department of Education (2010) estimates that approximately 6.7% of special education students ages 6 – 21 are identified as emotionally disturbed (Tibbets, 2013). However, estimates of children with ED varies greatly per state from a low of 1.5% in Arkansas to a high of 15.4% in Vermont (Tibbets, 2013). Some the main reasons cited for such variability in prevalence rates include:

Vague Criteria
- The definition for emotional disturbance is cited as convoluted, self-contradictory, and vague in nature leading educators to interpret criteria differently (Gresham, 2007; Merrell & Walker, 2004).

Low-Income
- Poverty tends to double the risk of a student being identified as ED (Costello, Messer, Bird, Cohen, & Reinherz, 1998).

Parent Involvement
- Some parents dislike the stigma of their child being labeled of ED, whereas others advocate for such a label to provide their child adequate services (Tibbets, 2013).

Race
- Often students coming from minority backgrounds are over identified as having ED (Green, 2012; National Education Association, 2008).

Gender
- Males are more likely to be identified as ED compared to females (Tibbets, 2013).

School Budget
- Schools may reduce the number of students identified as ED to stay within their budgets (Tibbets, 2013).

Proposed Alternative Definition for Emotional Disturbance?

To date, the best known alternative definition for Emotional Disturbance was developed and proposed by the National Mental Health and Special Education Coalition (Forness & Knitzer, 1992). In the definition, the term *Emotional or Behavior Disorder (EBD)* was used instead of *Emotional Disturbance* to recognize that emotional and behavior disorders may be internal or external in nature, and therefore eliminating the social maladjustment exclusionary clause (Forness & Knitzer, 1992). In 2005, the National Association of School Psychologists endorsed an adapted version of the original definition of Emotional or Behavior Disorders.

Of central difference to the original proposed definition for EBD and NASP's proposed definition is the inclusion of the identification of EBD being based on multiple sources of data about the individual's emotional or behavioral functioning. Both alternative definitions stress that a child with an emotional behavior disorder has a disability *that would persist in spite of increasingly intense interventions and supports within the general education setting.* In reference to increasingly intense interventions and multiple sources of data, both the original definition for EBD and NASP's adapted version appear to allude to the identification of an emotional or behavioral condition based on unresponsiveness to an MTSS intervention model. Figure 17 displays the original definition for ED and alternative definitions.

Emotional Disturbance Definition (IDEA, 2004; Adopted in 1975)

Emotional Disturbance means a condition exhibiting one or more of the following characteristics over a long period of time and to a marked degree that adversely affects a child's educational performance:

   i.   An inability to learn that cannot be explained by intellectual, sensory, or health factors.

      A.   An inability to build or maintain satisfactory interpersonal relationships with peers and teachers.

      B.   Inappropriate types of behavior or feelings under normal circumstances.

      C.   A general pervasive mood of unhappiness or depression.

      D.   A tendency to develop physical symptoms or fears associated with personal or school problems

   ii.   Emotional disturbance includes schizophrenia. The term does not apply to children who are socially maladjusted, unless it is determined that they have an emotional disturbance.

Original Emotional or Behavior Disorder Definition (Forness & Knitzer, 1992)

i.   The term Emotional or Behavior Disorder (EBD) means a disability characterized by behavioral or emotional responses in school so different from appropriate age, cultural, or ethnic norms that they adversely affect educational performance. Educational performance includes academic, social, vocational, and personal skills. Such a disability

      A.   Is more than a temporary, expected response to stressful events in the environment;

      B.   Is consistently exhibited in two different settings, at least one of which is school-related; and…

      C.   Is unresponsive to direct intervention in general education or the child's condition is such that general interventions would be insufficient.

ii.   Emotional and behavioral disorders can co-exist with other disabilities. This category may include children or youth with schizophrenic disorders, affective disorders, anxiety disorders or other sustained disturbances of conduct or adjustment when they adversely affect educational performance in accordance with section 1.

NASP Adapted Definition for Emotional or Behavior Disorder (NASP, 2005)

i. Emotional or Behavior Disorder (EBD) refers to a condition in which behavior or emotional responses of an individual in school are so different from his/her generally accepted, age appropriate, ethnic or cultural norms that the adversely affect performance in such areas as self-care, social relationships, personal adjustment, academic progress, classroom behavior, or work adjustment.

ii. EBD is more than a transient, expected response to stressors in the child's or youth's environment and would persist even with individualized interventions, such as feedback to the individual, consultation with parents or families and or modification of the educational environment.

iii. The identification of EBD must be based on multiple sources of data about the individual's behavioral or emotional functioning. EBD must be exhibited in at least two different settings, at least one of which is school related.

iv. EBD can co-exist with other disabilities.

Emotional Disturbance Definition (IDEA, 2004; Original Definition Proposed, 1975)	Proposed Emotional or Behavior Disorder Definition (Forness & Knitzer, 1992)	NASP Adapted Definition for Emotional or Behavior Disorder (National Association of School Psychologists, 2005)
Emotional Disturbance as a condition exhibiting one or more of the following characteristics over a long period of time and to a marked degree that adversely affects a child's educational performance: i. An inability to learn that cannot be explained by intellectual, sensory, or health factors. ii. An inability to build or maintain satisfactory interpersonal relationships with peers and teachers. iii. Inappropriate types of behavior or feelings under normal circumstances. iv. A general pervasive mood of unhappiness or depression. v. A tendency to develop physical symptoms or fears associated with personal or school problems Emotional disturbance includes schizophrenia. The term does not apply to children who are socially maladjusted, unless it is determined that they have an emotional disturbance. *Figure 17*	I) The term Emotional or Behavior Disorder (EBD) means a disability characterized by behavioral or emotional responses in school so different from appropriate age, cultural, or ethnic norms that they adversely affect educational performance. Educational performance includes academic, social, vocational, and personal skills. Such a disability D. Is more than a temporary, expected response to stressful events in the environment; E. Is consistently exhibited in two different settings, at least one of which is school-related; and F. Is unresponsive to direct intervention in general education or the child's condition is such that general interventions would be insufficient. II) Emotional and behavioral disorders can co-exist with other disabilities III) This category may include children or youth with schizophrenic disorders, affective disorders, anxiety disorders or other sustained disturbances of conduct or adjustment when they adversely affect educational performance in accordance with section 1.	v. Emotional or Behavior Disorder (EBD) refers to a condition in which behavior or emotional responses of an individual in school are so different from his/her generally accepted, age appropriate, ethnic or cultural norms that the adversely affect performance in such areas as self-care, social relationships, personal adjustment, academic progress, classroom behavior, or work adjustment. vi. EBD is more than a transient, expected response to stressors in the child's or youth's environment and would persist even with individualized interventions, such as feedback to the individual, consultation with parents or families and or modification of the educational environment. vii. The identification of EBD must be based on multiple sources of data about the individual's behavioral or emotional functioning. EBD must be exhibited in at least two different settings, at least one of which is school related. viii. EBD can co-exist with other disabilities.

CLICK HERE TO PLAY IMPORTANCE OF MENTAL HEALTH VIDEO

What is Social-Emotional MTSS?

Due to many districts lacking a true continuum of services for students with emotional difficulties, these children continue to be underserved and under-identified (Merrell and Walker, 2004). Without effective early intervention, children displaying social, emotional, and/or behavioral deficits are at significant risk for poor academic achievement, school dropout, conduct problems, antisocial behavior, delinquency, financial hardship, and serious mental health concerns (Daly, Nicholls, Aggarwal, & Sander, 2014). As recognition for schools becoming "de facto" mental health centers grows, many districts have been taxed with how to outline an MTSS model for students experiencing emotional difficulties. Despite emotional and behavioral multi-tiered systems of support being in the infancy stages, Gresham, 2007 outlined four advantages of schools adopting a multi-tiered system of support for identifying students with emotional and behavioral disorders of which include:

1) Early identification of emotional and behavioral deficits leading to more effective interventions.

2) Conceptualization of emotional and behavioral difficulties in terms of a risk rather than a deficit model. In other words, students are identified as being "at-risk" for developing an

emotional or behavioral disability through screening and attempting evidence-based interventions to remediate areas of concern. This model differs from the traditional model of practice in which students tended to be faulted as having irreversible deficits that cannot be changed (Gresham, 2007).

3) Reduction of identification biases and over-identification of minority groups.

4) Focus is placed on student outcomes. Emphasis is placed on the assessment of "measurable and changeable aspects of the instructional environment that are related to student outcomes (Gresham, 2007).

One additional advantage of servicing students with emotional and behavioral difficulties under an MTSS model is that such a model may save districts and society money. It is estimated that for every dollar spent on child behavioral health services, at least $2, and up to $10, is saved (in more intensive service such as social services, Juvenile Justice, and lost productivity) (Lever, Castle, Bernstein, Conners, & Bizzard, 2015).

Emotional and behavioral health disorders among children cost the United States taxpayers $247 billion annually in mental health services, lost productivity, and crime (Lever, Castle, Berstein, Sharma, & Blizzard, 2015).

In light of all the advantages offered through an MTSS model for social-emotional disorders, districts should strongly consider the adoption of such a model to best serve and identify students at-risk for developing mental health concerns and those children with a true emotional disturbance. Ultimately, a student's failure to respond to increasingly intense interventions, suggests that the child has an emotional disturbance and should qualify for special education services. Although literature is still emerging on development of a social-emotional MTSS model, a proposed outline can be found below.

Tier 1

Tier 1 of social-emotional MTSS focuses on the promotion of mental wellness in the schools for all students and how mental illness can negatively affect student learning and growth in the emotional, social, and behavioral domains (National Association of School Psychologists, 2015). Central to promoting social-emotional wellness in the schools is the training of school staff on the warning signs of mental health concerns and the importance of maintaining a healthy and structured school environment. A collaboration and designation of roles between school psychologists, school counselors, and school social workers may best assist in developing a healthy and welcoming school climate that takes into account each practices understanding of mental wellness and how to best promote mental health in the schools. A formation of such a team of mental health practitioners may greatly assist in devising in-service trainings in regards to childhood mental health and wellness.

Under the direction of the school-based mental health team, consultation can be provided to teachers to facilitate social-emotional learning in their classroom curriculum (National Association of School Psychologists, 2015). For example, the school-based mental health team may provide the teacher with consultation over how bullying can impact a child's social-emotional well-being and prevent them from accessing the learning environment. Additionally, the mental health team can assist administrators in developing disciplinary policies and procedures that are culturally responsive and avoid disproportionate application to specific populations (National Association of School Psychologists, 2015, p. 3). Critical to the formation of the school-based mental health team is utilization of the school psychologist beyond their traditional role of "gatekeeper for special education" and "tester." Schools Psychologist's expertise in counseling, consultation, research, and program evaluation should be employed to best promote social-emotional preventive practices.

At the Tier 1 Level, school psychologists may address system-wide issues related to bullying prevention, stress reduction, prosocial life skills, character values, and provide incidental counseling/consulting (Beaulieu & Sulkowski, 2015). For example, a school psychologist may briefly counsel a student who is having a disagreement with a peer or push into a classroom and teach students strategies for reducing test anxiety. Additionally, school psychologists may dedicate considerable time in universally screening students for mental health concerns, develop local norms for such screening, and utilize screening data to evaluate the effectiveness of school-wide social-emotional programs (National Association of School Psychologists, 2015). Screening for social-emotional concerns should occur three-times per year. Students who fall below the 25th percentile on screening measures are considered at-risk for displaying social-emotional concerns and should receive Tier 2 interventions. Students who fall below the 10th percentile are considered extremely at-risk for developing or having social or emotional concerns.

Specific Tier 1 programs for promoting social, emotional, and behavioral wellness include The Incredible Years, PATHS, Good Behavior Game, PATHS to Pax, Social Emotional Foundations of Early Learning (SEFEL), and Second Step. The focus of these programs is to reduce common risk factors students face in developing social, emotional, and behavioral concerns. Figure 18 provides an overview of the aforementioned programs. A more comprehensive evaluation of Tier 1 social, emotional, and behavioral programs can be found in Evidence-Based School Mental Health Services: Affect Education, Emotion Regulation Training, and Cognitive Behavioral Therapy (Macklem, 2011) and Handbook of School Mental Health: Research, Training, and Policy, 2nd Edition (Daly, Nicholls, Aggarwal, & Sander, 2014). Approximately, 80 to 85% of students are expected to respond to Tier 1 social-emotional programs.

Tier 2

Tier 2 of social-emotional MTSS is designed for the 15 – 20% of students who do not respond to Tier 1 school-wide mental and behavioral health programs. Tier II social-emotional programs, counseling, and activities offer a higher level of support from various school-based mental health practitioners (Livanis, Mulligan, Florin, and Mougrabi, 2012). Many Tier 2 programs, such as The Incredible Years (IY), incorporate and train parents, teachers, and/or community members to provide increased support for children who are experiencing the beginning symptoms of various internalizing and/or externalizing disorders (Livanis et al., 2012).

At the Tier 2 level, school psychologists may provide parents, teachers, and administrators' strategies for assisting students at-risk for social-emotional concerns (Livanis et al., 2012; National Association of School Psychologists, 2015). Additionally, school psychologists may provide group counseling and consultation for students with emphasis being placed on social skills training, self-esteem building exercises, conflict resolution strategies, and general cognitive-behavioral techniques such as identifying and regulating negative emotional states (Beaulieu & Sulkowski, 2015). For example, a school psychologist may provide group cognitive-behavioral therapy sessions to assist students with stress management (Joyce-Beaulieu & Sulkowski, 2015). Counseling sessions at the Tier 2 level are less individualized and tend to address broader rather than specific problems experienced by students. Tier 2 services are designed as short-term and low intensity interventions that may or may not be structured around a prescribed curricula. Tier 2 services typically take place once or twice a week over the course of 6 to 12 weeks (Joyce-Beauliue & Sulkowski, 2015). Progress monitoring at the Tier 2 level should occur on a weekly or bi-weekly basis. Prescribed programs at the Tier 2 level include Skillstreaming and the Early Risers "Skills for Success" program.

Tier 3

Tier 3 services are designed for 1 to 5% of students with the most pervasive and severe social emotional concerns (Joyce-Beauliue & Sulkowski, 2015). These children have not responded adequately to primary or secondary levels of social-emotional support and require more formalized and extensive therapeutic approaches to address their areas of difficulty (Joyce-Beaulieue & Sulkowski, 2015). At this tier, supports and counseling sessions become more individualized, direct, and person-centered. These students may take part in both group and individual counseling, such as cognitive-behavioral or dialectal-behavioral therapy sessions, to assist in overcoming their social-emotional concerns (Livanis et al., 2012). Examples of Tier 3 counseling programs include Coping with Depression for Adolescents (CWD-A) and the Coping Power Programs.

A critical role of the school psychologist at Tier 3 level of social-emotional MTSS is the facilitation of collaboration between school and community mental and behavioral health providers (National Association of School Psychologists, 2015). At this tier, school psychologists should act as a vital liaison between the school and community helping to assist in the orchestration of wraparound services both inside and outside of the school. Development of counseling treatment plans and/or FBA/BIPs may need to be developed to specifically address the student's social, emotional, and/or behavioral concerns. Finally, school psychologists should assist teachers and administrators in designing specific instructional strategies and consider whether co-existing emotional disturbances may be preventing the child from benefiting adequately from instruction (Livanis et al., 2012). At the Tier 3 level, progress monitoring should take place on a weekly or even bi-weekly basis.

Click for an overview of social-emotional programs across the 3 Tiers

CLICK HERE FOR DBT VIDEO

CLICK HERE FOR CBT VIDEO

What Can Districts Use to Screen or Progress Monitor Student Mental Health?

Universal screening and progress monitoring tools for assessing student's social-emotional well-being are in their infancy stages. However, several measures are available that either address social-emotional functioning, behavior, or both. As awareness grows for school-wide mental health initiatives, additional screening and progress monitoring measures are to be developed and implemented. A brief description of such measures is provided in the following sections.

Behavior Intervention Monitoring Assessment System-2 (BIMAS-2)
5 – 10 Minute Universal Screener & Progress Monitoring

The Behavior Intervention Monitoring System (BIMAS) is a measure of social, emotional, behavioral, and academic functioning in children and adolescents between the ages of 5 to 18-years (Behavior Intervention Monitoring System, n. d.). The BIMAS has been designed as a three-tier social, emotional, and behavioral monitoring system for screening and assessing changes in response to intervention and program evaluation at the individual, group, class, grade, school, or district level (McDougal, Bardos, & Meier, n. d.). The five areas assessed by the BIMAS are conduct (anger management, bullying), negative affect (anxiety, depression), cognitive/attention (attention, focus, organization), social (social, communication), and academic functioning (academic performance, attendance, attitude towards learning). The BIMAS has two main components: BIMAS Standard and BIMAS Flex.

The BIMAS Standard consists of 34-change-sensitive items that were based on a "scientific model for item selection called Intervention Item Selection Rules" (Behavior Intervention Monitoring System, n. d. para. 1). The BIMAS provides a parallel set of items across three rater forms: Parent (34 items; 5 – 18 years), Teacher (34 items; 5 – 18 years); and Self-Report (12 – 18 years). A non-norm referenced clinician form is available for rating youth between 5 to 18 years (Behavior Intervention Monitoring Assessment System, n. d.).

The BIMAS Flex is an extension of the BIMAS and involves more specific behavioral items (10 – 30) for each of the 34 BIMAS Standard form items on the 5 scales (Behavior Intervention Monitoring System, n. d.). Through the BIMAS Flex clinicians can customize treatment goals by selecting behaviors of concern and develop a three-to-five item mini evaluation for frequent progress monitoring of a specific are of concern (Behavior Intervention Monitoring System, n. d.). Student progress monitoring through BIMAS Flex can take place by different raters across the parent, teacher, and self-report forms.

Student Internalizing Behavior Screener (SIBS)
Universal Screener

- The Student Internalizing Behavior Screener (SIBS) is a companion screener to the Student Risk Screening Scale (SRSS). Like the SRSS, the SIBS utilizes a four-point Likert rating scale to compare students across seven social-emotional risk factors for developing an internalizing behavior disorder (Cook, Wright, Gresham, & Burns, 2010). Teachers rate each student in the class on the following factors 1) nervous or fearful; 2) bullied by peers; 3) spends time alone; 4) low academic achievement; 5) withdrawn; 6) sad or unhappy; and 7) complains about being sick or hurt. Total scores on the SIBS range from 0 to 21. Scores from 0 to 3 indicate low-risk status. Scores from 4 to 7 indicate moderate risk and scores from 8 to 21 indicate high risk for internalizing concerns.

Behavior and Emotional Screening System (BESS)
5 – 10 Minute Universal Screener

- The Behavior and Emotional Screening System (BESS) is an extension of the Behavior Assessment System for Children; Third Edition (BASC-3). The BESS is a brief, universal screening instrument for measuring behavioral and emotional strengths and weaknesses in children and adolescents between the ages of 2 and 18 years of age (BASC-3 BESS, n. d.). More specifically, the BESS evaluates children and adolescents in the areas of internalizing problems, externalizing problems, school problems, and adaptive skills (BASC-3 BESS, n. d.). The BESS includes three forms, which can be used in combination with one another or separately: Teacher Form (2 – 18 years), Parent Form (2 – 18 years), and Student Self-Report Form (8 – 18 years). Spanish parent and self-Report forms available.

Social Skills Improvement System (SISS)
5 – 10 Minute Universal Screener 5 – 10 minutes

- The Social Skills Improvement System (SSIS) Rating Scale is a universal screener designed to assess children 3 to 18 years of age in the areas of social skills (communication, cooperation, empathy etc.), competing problem behaviors (externalizing, bullying, internalizing etc.), and academic competence (reading achievement, math achievement, and motivation to learn) (Social Skills Improvement System Rating Scales, n. d.). The SSIS Rating Scale is one component of the Social Skills Improvement System program designed to teach social skills to children. The SSIS Rating Scales comes in English and Spanish forms.

Review360 by AIMSweb
Universal Screener and Progress Monitoring System

- AIMSweb's Review360 is a new universal screening and progress monitoring system for identifying students at-risk for developing internalizing and externalizing disorders. Components of Review360 include the BESS and Social Skills Improvement System (AIMSweb Review360, n. d.). The seven behavior categories covered by Review360 include inattention-organization, hyperactivity-impulsivity, social deficiencies, defiance, aggression, academic problems, and self-concept (AIMSweb Review360, n. d.).

Devereux Student Strengths Assessment
(DESSA-Mini & DESSA)
1-Minute Universal Screener (DESSA-Mini) & Progress Monitoring

- The DESSA-Mini and DESSA form a comprehensive system utilized to screen, progress monitor, and evaluate social-emotional competence and resilience in children kindergarten – 8th grade (Devereux Center for Resilient Children, n. d). The DESSA-Mini takes approximately 1-minute to complete or one full-planning period to screen a whole class and is designed for universal screening purposes. The DESSA measures eight key social-emotional competencies and can be used for progress monitoring at the Tier 2 and Tier 3 levels (Devereux Center for Resilient Children, n. d). The DESSA assesses children's social-emotional competency across the following areas: self-awareness, self-management, social awareness, decision making, optimistic thinking, relationship skills, goal directed behavior, and personal responsibility.

Children's Depression Inventory-2 (CDI 2)
5 – 15 minutes Universal Screener and Progress Monitoring

- The Children's Depression Inventory 2 is a revision of the original CDI and comes in a standard and short form. The measure is designed to be used in both educational and clinical settings to evaluate the early identification of depressive symptoms in children and adolescents between 7 to 17 years of age (CDI 2, n. d.). More specifically the CDI 2 evaluates emotional and functional problems across five subscales: negative mood, negative self-esteem, ineffectiveness, and interpersonal problems (CDI 2, n. d.). The standard version of the CDI 2 comes in parent, teacher, and self-report forms and is designed to acquire a greater understanding of the child's depressive symptoms (CDI 2, n. d). The CDI 2 standard form can be administered in 5 to 15 minutes. The CDI 2 short form is designed to be a screening and progress monitoring measure (CDI 2, n. d.; Joyce-Beaulieu & Sulkowski, 2015). The CDI short form is only available as a self-report measure.

<u>*Beck Youth Inventories – Second Edition (BYI-II)*</u>
5 minutes per inventory

- The Beck Youth Inventories are five separate forms that assess youth between the ages of 7 and 18 years of age in the areas of depression, anxiety, anger, disruptive behavior, and self-concept (Beck Youth Inventories – Second Edition, n. d.). The five BYI-II forms are as follows: Depression Inventory, Anxiety Inventory, Anger Inventory, Disruptive Behavior Inventory, and Self-Concept Inventory. Each inventory takes approximately 5 minutes to complete.

Social-Emotional Programs Quick Reference

More detailed description and easy reference charts follow this section (Figure 18)

Tier 1

PROMOTING ALTERNATIVE THINKING STRATEGIES (PATHS):
- Program designed to promote social-emotional learning through assisting all students develop emotional understanding, self-control, social skills, and problem solving strategies.

GOOD BEHAVIOR GAME (GBG):
- The Good Behavior Game is classroom-based behavior management intervention for elementary school students. It has been found to reduce drug and alcohol use, criminal behavior, mental health concerns, and suicide in adolescents and young adults.

PATHS TO PAX (PATHS + GBG) – No Website
- An integrated model combining PATHS with the Good Behavior Game.

SECOND STEP:
- Set of classroom-based curricula that provide instruction in social-emotional learning.

Tier 1 or Tier 2

FRIENDS:
- Program that incorporates cognitive and behavioral strategies for children and adolescents at-risk for anxiety and depression. The program is endorsed by the World Health Organization.

INCREDIBLE YEARS:
- Set of evidence-based interlocking programs for teachers, parents, and children used to promote social, emotional, and academic competence.

PENN RESILIENCY PROGRAM:
- The Penn Resiliency Program (PRP) was designed to teach cognitive, behavioral, and social skills to children at risk for depression or to prevent symptoms of depression in children (Macklem, 2011).

Tier 2

POD-TEAMS DEPRESSION PREVENTION PROGRAM:
- The POD Teams Depression Prevention Program is a psycho-educational, cognitive behavioral intervention for preventing depression in adolescents who have an increased risk of depression.

SOCIAL ACADEMIC INTERVENITON GROUPS (SAIG):
- Intervention that is designed around the CIRCLE and Skillstreaming curriculums. Groups tend to focus on classroom survival skills and emotional management skills.

SKILLSTREAMING:
- Program designed to teach children social skills, dealing with feelings, alternatives to aggression, and coping with stress.

EARLY RISERS/SKILLS FOR SUCCESS:
- Program that targets kindergarten and first-grade students who are at high risk and/or are demonstrating early aggressive, disruptive, and oppositional behavior. No Website (Call University at Minnesota at 612-723-9711 to inquire about access to program).

SUPPORT FOR STUDENTS EXPOSED TO TRAUMA (SSET):
- A series of 10 support groups that are utilized to manage the distress that results from exposure to trauma.

Tier 3 (Group or Individualized Interventions)

COPING POWER PROGRAM:
- A cognitive-behavioral intervention for children at the elementary and middle school levels. The program focuses on self-regulation, social competence, and positive parental involvement (Macklem, 2011).

COPING WITH DEPRESSION FOR ADOLESCENTS (CWD-A) - FREE ONLINE:
- A cognitive, behavioral, social skills, and relaxation training-based program for actively depressed adolescents (Macklem, 2011).

COGNITIVE BEHAVIORAL INTERVENTION FOR TRAUMA IN SCHOOLS (CBITS):
- A group or individualized intervention used to reduce systems of trauma, Post-Traumatic Stress Disorder, depression, anxiety, and behavioral problems.

COPING CAT & THE C.A.T. PROJECT:
- The Coping Cat Program and its extension equivalent, the C.A.T. Project are Cognitive Behavior Therapy Treatment programs for children who exhibit anxiety disorders such as Separation Anxiety, Generalized Anxiety Disorder, and/or Social Phobia (Macklem, 2011).

Tier 3 (Non-standardized Group or Individualized Interventions)

COGNITIVE BEHAVIOR THERAPY (CBT) – No Official Website
Excellent CBT Resources can be found at <u>Psychologytools.com</u>
- CBT assists children in exploring their thoughts, feelings, and actions and how children may interpret situations (Mennuti & Christner, 2012).

DIALECTICAL BEHAVIOR THERAPY-ADOLESCENT (DBT-A) – No Website

- DBT-A was developed to target instability, mood liability, and difficult regulating emotions in adolescents experiencing depression, sadness, relationship issues, and school problems (Fiorillo & Long, 2012).

PATHS: Promoting Alternative Thinking Strategies Tier 1	
Age/Grade Range	Pre-K – 5th grade
Setting	Classroom
Length	Academic Year (131 twenty-minute lessons)
Facilitator	Teacher
Description & Website	Program designed to promote social-emotional learning through assisting all students develop emotional understanding, self-control, social skills, and problem solving strategies (Macklem, 2010). Students learn how to discuss basic feelings and feeling management. With special education students, the program has shown promise in reducing externalizing behaviors and depressive symptomology (Daly et al., 2014). **Website:** http://www.pathseducation.com/
Areas Targeted	✓ Social-Emotional Understanding ✓ Self-Control ✓ Problem Solving ✓ Feeling Recognition ✓ Feeling Management ✓ Aggression & Behavior problems ✓ Oppositional Behavior ✓ Conduct Problems ✓ Impulsivity & Hyperactivity

	Good Behavior Game Tier 1	
Age/Grade Range	1 – 6th grade (Typically 1st grade)	
Setting	Classroom	
Length	Academic Year (3 x's a wk. for 10 minutes Increases over time)	
Facilitator	Teacher	
Description & Website	The Good Behavior Game (GBG) is a classroom-based behavior management intervention for elementary school students. The game assigns students to teams that are balanced based on gender, disruptive behavior, and socially isolated behavior (Goodbehaviorgame.org). Classroom rules are posted and reviewed. Each team is rewarded if team members commit a total of four of fewer violations of the classroom rules during game periods. GBG has been found to reduce aggressive, off-task, and disruptive behavior. Additionally, GBG has been found to reduce drug and alcohol use, criminal behavior, mental health concerns, and suicide in adolescents and young adults (American Institute for Research, n.d.). **Website:** http://goodbehaviorgame.org/	
Areas Targeted	✓ Self-Regulation & Control ✓ Cooperation & Compliance ✓ Interpersonal Relations ✓ Socialization ✓ Oppositional Behavior	✓ Aggressive Behavior ✓ Disruptive Behaviors ✓ Shy/Reserved ✓ Social Isolation ✓ Risk for Suicide

PATHS to PAX (PATHS + Good Behavior Game) Tier 1	
Age/Grade Range	1 – 6th grade
Setting	Classroom
Length	Academic Year
Facilitator	Teacher
Description & Website	An integrated model combining PATHS with the Good Behavior Game. Implementing PATHS to PAX has resulted in reductions in internalizing and externalizing symptoms. **Website:** None
Areas Targeted	✓ Self-Regulation/Control ✓ Social-Emotional Understanding ✓ Feeling Recognition ✓ Feeling Management ✓ Interpersonal Relations ✓ Socialization ✓ Cooperation w/ Others ✓ Oppositional Behavior ✓ Conduct Problems ✓ Aggressive Behavior ✓ Disruptive Behaviors

	Second Step Tier 1	
Age/Grade Range	Pre-K – 8th grade	
Setting	Classroom	
Length	15 – 25 weeks (35 min. each)	
Facilitator	Teacher	
Description & Website	Second Step is a set of classroom-based curricula that provides instruction in social-emotional learning. Units focus on skill development in the areas of empathy, friendship skills, problem solving, and learning (Daly et al., 2014). Lessons involves songs, games, activities, videos, and take-home materials. A Spanish version of Second Step is available. **Website:** http://www.cfchildren.org/second-step	
Areas Targeted	✓ Attention & Listening ✓ Impulsive Behaviors ✓ Aggressive Behaviors ✓ Self-Talk & Metacognition ✓ Feeling Recognition ✓ Feeling Management	✓ Social Skills, Prosocial Behavior, & Interpersonal Relations ✓ Problem Solving ✓ Academic/Learning Skills

FRIENDS
Tier 1 & Tier 2

Age/Grade Range	4 yrs. – Adult
Setting	Classroom or pull-out group (3 – 6 students)
Length	Child Component 10 sessions 2 booster sessions (60 – 75 mins in length) Parent Component 6 hr. parent component (4 sessions) Sessions can be adapted as long as the sequence and structure are respected.
Facilitator	✓ Teacher ✓ School-Based Mental Health Professional ✓ Allied Health Professionals
Description & Website	One of the most supported programs for internalizing disorders. The program incorporates cognitive and behavioral strategies for children and adolescents at-risk for anxiety and depression and has also been utilized as a prevention program (Macklem, 2011). Parent training programs are an integral part of FRIENDS. The FRIENDS acronym stands for Feeling worried, Relax and feel good, Inner thoughts, Explore plans of actions, Nice work, Reward yourself, Don't forget to practice, and Stay cool. The FRIENDS program was designed to be delivered in both clinical and educational settings and has been shown to be effective with ESL students (Macklem, 2011). **Website:** https://www.friendsprograms.com/
Areas Targeted	✓ Feeling Recognition ✓ Socialization ✓ Feeling Management ✓ Resiliency Development ✓ Stress Management ✓ Parent Involvement/Training ✓ Interpersonal Relations

Incredible Years (IY): Parent, Teacher, and Child Training Series Tier 1 & 2	
Age/Grade Range	2 – 12 years
Setting	Classroom or pull-out group (3 – 6 students) Parent Groups
Length	<u>Child Program</u> <u>Parent Program</u> 18 – 22 wks. 12 – 20 wks. 2 hr. sessions (2 – 3 hr. sessions)
Facilitator	Teacher or School-Based Mental Health Professional
Description & Website	Set of evidence-based interlocking programs for teachers, parents, and children used to promote social, emotional, and academic competence. The Tier 1 aspect of program is designed to prevent and diminish oppositional behaviors such as defiance, hostility, and aggression. Program teaches caregivers parenting strategies and children empathy, social skills, and anger management. The Tier 2 aspect of the program consists of 60 pull-out lessons and small group activities for students already demonstrating defiance, opposition, or aggression. **Website:** http://incredibleyears.com/
Areas Targeted	✓ Oppositional Behavior ✓ Social, Emotional, & Competency ✓ Conduct Problems ✓ Academic/Learning Skills ✓ Antisocial Behavior ✓ Parent Involvement/Training ✓ Aggressive Behavior ✓ Internal Problems such as ✓ Anger Management depression

Penn Resiliency Program
Tier 1 & 2

Age/Grade Range	10 – 14 years
Setting	Classroom (15 – 30 students) Small Group (3 – 6 Students)
Length	12- 90 minute lessons or 18 - 60 –minute lessons
Facilitator	School-Based Mental Health Professional
Description & Website	The Penn Resiliency Program (PRP) was designed to teach cognitive, behavioral, and social skills to children at-risk for depression or to prevent symptoms of depression in children (Macklem, 2011). The model utilizes Albert Ellis' ABC model which stresses that our beliefs about events impact our emotions and behavior (Macklem, 2011). The program's main goal is to prevent and decrease depressive thinking patterns and promote resiliency. Skills are taught through games, discussions, role plays, cartoons, and short stories. Studies have also shown some positive effects in reducing anxiety (Gillham, Reivich, & Seligman, n.d.). **Website:** http://www.positivepsychology.org/research/resilience-children
Areas Targeted	✓ Depression ✓ Anxiety ✓ Emotional Competency ✓ Social Competency ✓ Feeling Recognition ✓ Feeling Management ✓ Coping ✓ Decision Making ✓ Problem Solving

POD-Teams Depression Prevention Program
Tier 2

Age/Grade Range	13 – 17 years
Setting	Pull-Out Group (4 – 8 Students)
Length	8 Ninety-Minute Weekly Sessions
Facilitator	School-Based Mental Health Practitioner
Description & Website	The POD Teams Depression Prevention Program is a psycho-educational, cognitive behavioral intervention for preventing depression in adolescents who have an increased risk of depression (TEAMS/POD Intervention Team, 2003). The program is not designed for students who are currently in an active depression episode. The POD Teams Depression Prevention Program was designed for adolescents who already carry some known increased risk of depression, such as having a past episode of depression, having depressed parents, and/or reporting dysphoria (TEAMS/POD Intervention Team, 2003). For students suffering from an active episode of depression, the Coping with Depression for Adolescents Program or individual cognitive-behavioral therapy is recommended. **Website:** https://www.kpchr.org/research/public/acwd/acwd.html **Free Materials and Manual Online!**
Areas Targeted	✓ Past Episodes of Sadness ✓ Coping ✓ Dysphoria ✓ Problem-Solving ✓ Low Self-Esteem ✓ Social Withdrawal ✓ Parents w/ Past Depression

	Social Academic Intervention Groups (SAIG) **Tier 2**
Age/Grade Range	K - 8
Setting	Pull-Out Group (3 – 6 students)
Length	9 weeks
Facilitator	Teacher or School-Based Mental Health Practitioner)
Description & Website	SAIG groups are based on the Circle formant (where children sit in a circle to build a sense of belongingness) and restorative practices (Social Academic Instructional Group Curriculum, n. d.). Much of SAIG group's format relies heavily on *Skillstreaming* (Social Academic Instructional Group Curriculum, n. d.). There are two group themes to SAIG: Classroom Survival Skills and Emotional Management Skills. Classroom Survival Skills involve lessons that teach listening skills, following instructions, ignoring distractions, making corrections, and accepting consequences, and school absenteeism. Emotional Management Skills involve lessons in feeling recognition, relaxing, expression of feelings, and coping with anger. **Website: http://mps.milwaukee.k12.wi.us/en/Families/Family-Services/Intervention---PBIS/SAIG-Curriculum.htm**
Areas Targeted	✓ Academic Improvement (Following Directions, Asking for Help) ✓ Academic skills ✓ Learning Skills ✓ School Absenteeism ✓ Educational and Professional Aspirations ✓ Emotional & Behavioral Recognition and Self-Regulation ✓ Emotional Coping Techniques ✓ Expression of Feelings

	Skillstreaming **Tier 2**
Age/Grade Range	Pre-K - 12
Setting	Pull-Out Group (3 – 6 students)
Length	40 – 60 lessons/skills (# of lessons varies per age/grade level)
Facilitator	School-Based Mental Health Professional
Description & Website	Skillstreaming involves a four-part training approach that involves role-playing, modeling, performance feedback, and generalization to teach prosocial skills in the areas of social skills, dealing with feelings, alternatives to aggression, and coping with stress (Skillstreaming, n.d.) **Website:** http://www.skillstreaming.com/
Areas Targeted	✓ Social Skills & Interpersonal Relations ✓ Coping with feelings ✓ Feeling Recognition & Regulation ✓ Coping with Stress ✓ Anger/Aggression Management

	Early Risers "Skills for Success" **Tier 2**
Age/Grade Range	6 – 12 years (K – 1st Grade)
Setting	Pull-Out Group (4 – 6 students)
Length	Academic Year or 6 week Summer Program
Facilitator	Teacher or School-Based Mental Health Practitioner
Description & Website	Early Risers "Skills for Success" targets kindergarten and first-grade students who are at high risk and/or are demonstrating early aggressive, disruptive, and oppositional behavior (Daly et. al, 2014). The program applies both child and family focused interventions (Daly et al., 2014). The Child School component focuses on identifying areas of difficulties in the classroom and creates individualized plans to address those difficulties. The Parent Skills component is intended to promote parents' abilities to support their child's positive growth in the social, emotional, and behavioral domains (Daly et al, 2014). **Website:** None **Phone:** (612) 273-9711 University of Minnesota
Areas Targeted	✓ Emotional Self-Regulation ✓ Behavioral Self-Regulation ✓ Pro-Social Behavior, Social Skills & Interpersonal Relations ✓ Academic Skills ✓ Learning Skills ✓ Family Relationships ✓ Parent Training (Effective Discipline Practices, Parent Involvement in the school)

Support for Students Exposed to Trauma (SSET)
Tier 2

Age/Grade Range	10 -14 years *May be useful for students (as low as grade 4 or up to grade 9), but has not been used in those populations yet.*
Setting	Pull-Out Group (8 – 10 students)
Length	10 one-hour lessons
Facilitator	Teacher or School-Based Mental Health Professional
Description & Website	The Support for Students Exposed to Trauma (SSET) Program is a series of ten support groups that are utilized to manage the distress that results from exposure to trauma (Support for Students Exposed to Trauma, n. d.). SSET includes skill-building techniques to ameliorate anxiety, depressed mood, and stressors by writing or drawing about their traumatic experiences to process their emotions (Support for Students Exposed to Trauma, n. d.). **Websites:** 1) **https://traumaawareschools.org/sset** 2) **http://www.rand.org/content/dam/rand/pubs/technical_reports/2009/RAND_TR675.pdf**
Areas Targeted	✓ Trauma ✓ Nervousness ✓ PTSD ✓ Acting out ✓ Depression ✓ Impulsive or Risky Behavior ✓ Low Mood ✓ Resiliency ✓ Anxiety

	Coping Power Program Tier 3
Age/Grade Range	4th – 6th Grade
Setting	Pull-Out Group (4 – 6 students)
Length	<u>Child Component</u> 15 – 18 months (34 Cognitive-Behavioral Group Sessions) <u>Parent Component</u> 16 Group Sessions
Facilitator	School-Based Mental Health Professional
Description & Website	A cognitive-behavioral intervention for children at the elementary and middle school levels. The program focuses on self-regulation, social competence, and positive parental involvement (Macklem, 2011). **Website:** http://www.copingpower.com/Default.aspx
Areas Targeted	✓ Emotional Self-Regulation ✓ Behavioral Self-Regulation ✓ Aggressive Behaviors ✓ Social Skills ✓ Interpersonal Relations ✓ Entry into positive peer groups ✓ Organization/ ✓ Study Skills ✓ Academic/Learning Skills ✓ Parent Training (Praise, positive attention, child study skills).

Coping with Depression for Adolescents (CWD-A)
Tier 3

Age/Grade Range	9 – 18 years
Setting	Pull-Out Group (4 – 8 Students) After-School Group Sessions (4 – 8 Students)
Length	16 weekly two- hour sessions (8 weeks)
Facilitator	School-Based Mental Health Professional *To be used in consultation w/ outside clinicians.
Description & Website	The Coping with Depression for Adolescent Program is a cognitive, behavioral, social skills, and relaxation training-based program for actively depressed adolescents (Macklem, 2011). Adolescents are taught several skills to relieve depression and gain control when feeling negative by resolving conflict and changing maladaptive thinking (Macklem, 2011). A parent component assist in keeping parents aware of what their children are learning in the program. **Website:** https://www.kpchr.org/research/public/acwd/acwd.html
Areas Targeted	✓ Depression ✓ Problem Solving ✓ Conflict Resolution ✓ Planning for the Future ✓ Social Skills ✓ Social Withdrawal ✓ Prosocial Behavior ✓ Anhedonia ✓ Coping Skills ✓ Low Self-Esteem ✓ Relaxation ✓ Parent Involvement ✓ Mood Monitoring

	Cognitive Behavioral Intervention for Trauma in Schools (CBITS) Tier 3	

Age/Grade Range	10 – 15 years (5 – 9th grade)	
Setting	Pull-Out Group (8 – 10 students)	
Length	Pull-Out Group Sessions (8 – 10 Students) 1 – 3 individual Sessions 2 Parent Training Sessions 1 Teacher Educational Session	
Facilitator	School-Based Mental Health Professional	
Description & Website	The Cognitive Behavior Intervention for Trauma in Schools (CBITS) is a group and individual intervention used to reduce symptoms of trauma, Post-Traumatic Stress Disorder (PTSD), depression, anxiety, and behavioral problems (Cognitive Behavioral Intervention for Trauma in Schools, n. d.). CBITS has been used with students who have witnessed or experienced traumatic life events such as community and school violence, injuries and accidents, natural and man-made disasters, and physical and domestic violence (Cognitive Behavioral Intervention in Schools, n. d.). CBITS uses a variety of cognitive-behavioral techniques to assist children coping with trauma, anxiety, and depression such as psycho-education, cognitive restructuring, social problem solving, resiliency training, and exposure (Cognitive Behavioral Intervention for Trauma in Schools, n. d.). **Website:** 1) https://traumaawareschools.org/cbits 2) http://www.rand.org/content/dam/rand/pubs/technical_reports/2010/RAND_TR772.pdf	
Areas Targeted	✓ Trauma ✓ PTSD ✓ Cognitive Restructuring ✓ Depression/Low Mood	✓ Anxiety/Nervousness ✓ Acting out Behavior ✓ Social Problem Solving ✓ Parent Involvement

Coping Cat & The C.A.T Project
Tier 3

Age/Grade Range	Coping Cat: (7 – 13 years) The C.A.T. Project (14 – 17 years)
Setting	Pull-Out Group (4 to 5 Students)
Length	16 weeks (50 – 60 Minute Sessions)
Facilitator	School-Based Mental Health Professional
Description & Website	The Coping Cat Program and its age extension equivalent, The C. A. T. Project, are Cognitive-Behavioral Therapy treatment programs for children who exhibit anxiety disorders such as Separation Anxiety, Generalized Anxiety Disorder, and/or Social Phobia (Macklem, 2011). The programs utilize parents/family members as coaches to assist in treatment and arrange play-dates (Macklem, 2011). The program uses modeling, exposure, modeling, in-vivo exposure, role playing, relaxation, and relaxation to assist students in recognizing symptoms of their anxiety and overcoming it. **Website:** http://www.workbookpublishing.com/product_info.php?products_id=30
Areas Targeted	✓ Anxiety Disorders ✓ Parent Involvement ✓ Feeling Recognition ✓ Physical Recognition ✓ Anxiety Exposure/ Desensitization ✓ Regulation of Anxiety ✓ Coping Skills ✓ Relaxation

	Cognitive-Behavior Therapy *(Non-manualized/Standardized)* Tier 3 (1 on 1 or Very Small Group Counseling; 2 – 3 students)	
Age/Grade Range	All Ages **1:1 counseling may offer the most intensive and specific level of intervention for non-responders	
Setting	Pull-Out Individualized or Group Sessions	
Length	10 – 20 weekly or bi-weekly sessions 50 – 60 minute sessions	
Facilitator	School Psychologist	
Description & Website	Cognitive-behavior therapy assists children in exploring their thoughts, feelings, and actions and how children may interpret situations (Mennuti & Christner, 2012). CBT helps children become aware of how their thoughts ultimately influenced his or her behavioral or emotional functioning (Mennuti & Christner, 2012). CBT combines cognitive and behavioral perspectives to assist youth in overcoming their deficits. **Website:** None **Books:** *Cognitive Behavior Therapy in K – 12 School Settings: A Practitioner's Toolkit* by Diana Joyce-Beaulieu and Michael L. Sulkowski *Cognitive-Behavioral Interventions in Educational Settings: A Handbook for Practice, Second Edition* Edited by Rosemary B. Mennuti, Ray W. Christner, and Arthur Freeman	
Areas Targeted	✓ Anxiety Disorders ✓ Nervousness ✓ Depression ✓ Sadness ✓ Phobias ✓ Fears ✓ Attention & Impulsivity	✓ Attention & Impulsivity ✓ Cognitive and Behavioral Restructuring ✓ Emotional and Behavioral Recognition and Regulation ✓ Coping Skills

Dialectical Behavior Therapy- Adolescent (DBT-A) *(Non-manualized/Standardized)* **Tier 3**	
Age/Grade Range	Adolescent – Young Adult
Setting	Pull-Out Individualized or Group Sessions
Length	16 weeks 50 – 60 Minutes Sessions
Facilitator	School Psychologist
Description & Website	Dialectical Behavior Therapy was originally developed and used for treating female outpatients diagnosed with Borderline Personality Disorder (Fiorillo & Long, 2012). It has since developed a growing evidence base for treating adolescent problem behaviors including self-injurious behavior, oppositional defiant disorder, learning disabilities, sadness, and depression. DBT was adapted from Cognitive Behavioral Therapy. DBT-A was developed to target instability, mood liability, and difficulty regulating emotions in adolescents experiencing depression, sadness, relationship issues, and school problems (Fiorillo & Long, 2012). **Website:** None
Areas Targeted	✓ Anxiety Disorders ✓ Cognitive and Behavioral ✓ Suicidal Adolescents Restructuring ✓ Self-Harm ✓ Emotional and Behavioral ✓ Depression/Sadness Recognition and Regulation ✓ Phobias ✓ Coping Skills ✓ Fears ✓ Oppositional Behaviors ✓ Parent Involvement

Figure 19   ***Social-Emotional Flow Chart***

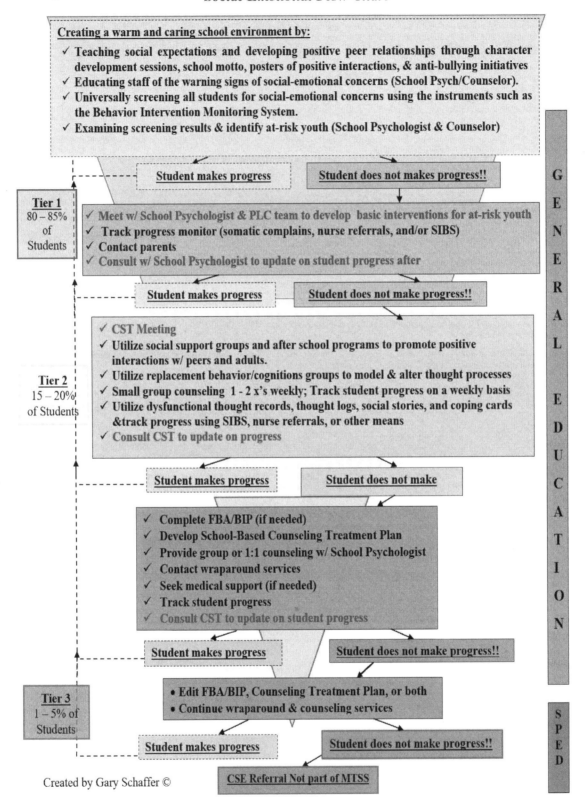

Creating a warm and caring school environment by:
- ✓ Teaching social expectations and developing positive peer relationships through character development sessions, school motto, posters of positive interactions, & anti-bullying initiatives
- ✓ Educating staff of the warning signs of social-emotional concerns (School Psych/Counselor).
- ✓ Universally screening all students for social-emotional concerns using the instruments such as the Behavior Intervention Monitoring System.
- ✓ Examining screening results & identify at-risk youth (School Psychologist & Counselor)

G E N E R A L   E D U C A T I O N

Student makes progress

Student does not makes progress!!

Tier 1
80 – 85%
of
Students

- ✓ Meet w/ School Psychologist & PLC team to develop basic interventions for at-risk youth
- ✓ Track progress monitor (somatic complains, nurse referrals, and/or SIBS)
- ✓ Contact parents
- ✓ Consult w/ School Psychologist to update on student progress after

Student makes progress

Student does not make progress!!

- ✓ CST Meeting
- ✓ Utilize social support groups and after school programs to promote positive interactions w/ peers and adults.
- ✓ Utilize replacement behavior/cognitions groups to model & alter thought processes
- ✓ Small group counseling 1 - 2 x's weekly; Track student progress on a weekly basis
- ✓ Utilize dysfunctional thought records, thought logs, social stories, and coping cards &track progress using SIBS, nurse referrals, or other means
- ✓ Consult CST to update on progress

Tier 2
15 – 20%
of Students

Student makes progress

Student does not make

- ✓ Complete FBA/BIP (if needed)
- ✓ Develop School-Based Counseling Treatment Plan
- ✓ Provide group or 1:1 counseling w/ School Psychologist
- ✓ Contact wraparound services
- ✓ Seek medical support (if needed)
- ✓ Track student progress
- ✓ Consult CST to update on student progress

Student makes progress

Student does not make progress!!

Tier 3
1 – 5% of
Students

- • Edit FBA/BIP, Counseling Treatment Plan, or both
- • Continue wraparound & counseling services

Student makes progress

Student does not make progress!!

S P E D

CSE Referral Not part of MTSS

Created by Gary Schaffer ©

Suicide Prevention Multi-Tiered Support

What is the Prevalence of Suicide in Youth Nationally and in NYS?

In New York State, suicide is the leading cause of death for children between 10 to 14 years of age and the fourth leading cause of death for youth between 15 to 19 years of age (NYS Department of Health, 2011). The act of committing suicide represents only one component among a continuum of suicidal behaviors that include suicidal ideation, communicating desires to commit suicide (making suicide plans or threats), and attempting suicide (Miller, 2014). Nationally, the Centers for Disease Control and Prevention (2013) reports that suicide is the second-leading cause of death in the United States among young people between 10 to 24 years of age. Due to suicide remaining a serious threat to the safety and security of young people, schools have often been viewed as a critical venue in focusing suicide prevention efforts (Miller, 2014).

"In 2013, 17% of United States high school students seriously considered suicide and 8% made an attempt" (National Association of School Psychologists, 2015).

Do Schools Have a Legal and Ethical Responsibility to Assist in Suicide Prevention and Intervention Efforts?

The simple answer to the question above is "yes." Schools appear to have a legal and ethical responsibility to prevent suicide whenever possible (Miller, 2014). Miller, 2014 writes that "school districts, as well as school personnel, can and have been sued in situations in which a student has died by suicide" (p. 15). Despite school personnel questioning whether they are appropriate providers of suicide prevention and intervention efforts, schools provide the majority of mental health services to children across the United States (Mazza & Reynolds, 2008; Miller, 2014). Additionally, school personnel have a duty to assist in preventing and protecting students from threatening harm to themselves or others (Miller, 2014). Therefore, schools have legal and ethical responsibilities in preventing suicide. Although, literature suggests that school districts develop a three tier model for suicide prevention and intervention, they are not legally or ethically required to develop and implement such programs (Miller, 2014). Nonetheless, schools remain an obvious place to deliver such preemptive curriculums and with increasing mental health demands being placed on educators, it would be in a district's best interest to develop a three-tiered model for suicide prevention and intervention (Balaguru, Sharma, & Waheed, 2013; Katz, et al., 2013; Miller, 2014).

97

Why are Schools Considered "Obvious" Places to Deliver Suicide Prevention Efforts?

As discussed, 70 to 80% of children receive mental health services in schools (National Association of School Psychologists, 2015). Two of the primary reasons cited for schools being considered "obvious" places to deliver suicide prevention efforts include children spending a significant amount of their time in relatively stable school environments and the ongoing lack of clinicians with expertise in preventing and intervening in children with mental health care needs (BAL guru et al., 2013; Miller, 2014). In rural areas of the country, the shortage of mental health care providers becomes even more apparent. For example, Seneca County in New York State has only 1 licensed psychologist (New York State Education Department Office of Professions, 2017). Therefore, rural districts like those in Seneca County, are especially taxed in providing services for children with mental health care needs and utilizing school-based mental health practitioners to do so. Additional reasons for schools being ideal in delivering suicide and mental health prevention and intervention efforts can be found on the following page.

In New York State, suicide is the leading cause of death for children between 10 to 14 years of age and the fourth leading cause of death for youth between 15 to 19 years of age (NYS Department of Health, 2011).

Reasons Schools are Ideal Places to Provide Mental Health and Suicide Prevention and Intervention Efforts:

- ✓ Children and adolescents spend the majority of their time in schools (Balaguru et al., 2013).

- ✓ 70 – 80% children receive mental health services through school-based mental health practitioners (National Association of School Psychologists, 2015).

- ✓ Schools provide a relatively stable and predictable environment where school-based mental health practitioners, such as school psychologists, can be readily accessed to provide counseling and immediate support (Balaguru et al., 2013; Miller, 2014).

- ✓ For outside clinicians and agencies, scheduling problems and wait lists prevent early intervention for youth at-risk for suicide or mental health concerns.

- ✓ Even if the outside clinician is accepting new child patients, wait time is usually 12 weeks or longer (Scharf et al., 2015). Often this time period is "too late" for many youth experiencing mental health concerns.

- ✓ For children in rural and impoverished communities, transportation and travel time to receive critical mental health support may not be ideal. Drive time may inhibit the child and caregiver's follow-up on future appointments due to lack of convenience.

- ✓ 80 – 90% of critical brain development takes place between birth and age 5 (Scharf et al., 2015). For students predisposed to mental illness or suicidal risk factors, early preventative remediation efforts are needed before brain development is hindered (Scharf et al., 2015).

- ✓ Strong relationships are formed with peers and school personnel to provide at-risk youth a system of interpersonal support during times of crisis (Miller, 2014). These systems of support can be mobilized quickest in the school setting.

For outside clinicians and agencies, scheduling problems and wait lists prevent early intervention for youth at-risk for suicide or mental health concerns. Even if the outside clinician is accepting new child patients, wait time is usually 12 weeks or longer (Scharf et al., 2015).

80 – 90% of critical brain development takes place between birth and age 5 (Scharf et al., 2015). For students predisposed to mental illness or suicidal risk factors, early preventative remediation efforts are needed before brain development is hindered (Scharf et al., 2015).

Are Schools Prepared to Provide Suicide Prevention and Intervention Efforts?

Although schools are ideal places to provide a three-tiered model for suicide prevention and intervention, many schools and school personnel remain underprepared and undereducated on mental health and suicide intervention efforts (Miller, 2014). Additionally, little research and evidence exists in evaluating the use of school-based suicide prevention and intervention programs for at-risk youth (Balaguru et. al., 2013; Katz et. al., 2013). With school-based mental health initiatives in schools in their developmental stages, a hard outline for school districts to implement a three-tiered model for suicide prevention and intervention is still emerging. Still, elements of an MTSS model for suicide prevention and intervention have been proposed by the National Association of School Psychologists (2015) and Miller (2014). Miller (2014) suggests that mental-health practitioners, such as school psychologists and counselors, "should be leaders in developing, implementing, and evaluating school-based suicide prevention programs" (p. 16). School Psychologists knowledge in the areas of mental health, preventative practice, program development, data-based decision making, counseling, and consultation practices make them ideal candidates for working with administrators, school counselors, and outside clinicians in the development of suicide prevention and intervention programs under an MTSS framework.

What Does Suicide Prevention and Intervention in an MTSS Model Look Like?

Like social-emotional MTSS, suicide prevention and intervention MTSS remains in its early stages. Still, there is much promise for implementing a three-tiered suicide prevention and intervention model in school districts. Some of the advantages of implementing such a model include developing a stringent outline for cohesively addressing suicide prevention and intervention efforts, familiarizing all school staff and students with signs of suicide and severe depression, screening for mental illness and suicidal risk factors, utilizing school-based mental health practitioners more effectively, and ensuring that effective communication is established between school and outside clinicians (Miller, 2014; Lieberman et al., 2008).

<u>Risk Factors and Signs of Youth Suicide</u>	<u>Protective Factors from Youth Suicide</u>
• **Mental Health:** Depressive disorders, substance abuse or dependence, anxiety disorders, personality disorders, difficulty regulating emotions, external locus of control	• **Mental Health:** Emotional well-being, internal locus of control, resilience, coping skills, ability to perceive, understand, and manage emotions.
• **Personal Characteristics:** Hopelessness, low self-esteem, loneliness, impulsivity, self-injurious behavior, bullied at school, risky sexual behavior, delinquency, low frustration tolerance, having a disability, withdrawn, lonely, anxious, fearful, & non-adaptable temperament.	• **Personal Characteristics:** Hopeful, good social and communication skills, close friends, connected to others, good self-esteem, adaptable temperament, frustration tolerance and emotional regulation, involved in positive outside activities, clubs, and/or sports
• **Family History:** Parent suicide or suicidal behavior or parental mental health problems, parent divorce, death of parent or close relative, problems in parent/child Relationship	• **Family History:** Little or no history of parental suicide or mental health problems, parents married or maintained amicable relationship, family support or connectedness to family, strong relationships with parents and parental involvement
• **Interpersonal Problems:** Difficulty getting along w/ others at school, work, or in the community	• **Interpersonal Relations:** Gets along and maintains relationships with others at school, work, or in the community
• **Access:** Access to firearms, medications, jumping sites (rooftops and buildings), drugs, or alcohol.	• **Access:** No or restricted access to firearms, medications, jumping sites (rooftops and buildings), drugs or alcohol.
Figure 17	Adapted from Center for Mental Health Services, Substance Abuse and Mental Health Services Administration (SAMHSA) (2012). *Preventing suicide: A toolkit for high schools* (HHS Publication No. 02-2650).

Figure 17

Tier 1 Prevention Efforts:

Tier I efforts for preventing suicide involve identifying at-risk youth and educating staff, students, and parents of the warning signs of suicidal behavior (Lieberman Poland, Cassel, 2008; Miller, 2014). Topics addressed at the Tier 1 level should contain dispelling common myths and misunderstandings about suicide, demographic information about suicide, discussing risk factors, warning signs, and protective factors, and informing school personnel and parents about community mental health supports/resources that are available. (Center for Mental Health Services: Substance Abuse and Mental Health Services Administration, 2012; Miller, 2014).

Although research is limited on Tier 1 programs, a prevention program that targets middle and high school youth is the Signs of Suicide Program. The Sings of Suicide program aims to raise teen's awareness of depressive and suicidal symptoms along with increasing their knowledge of how to appropriately seek help from adults (Katz et al., 2013; Lieberman et al., 2008). The program raises awareness in youth for depressive and suicidal symptoms by utilizing gatekeeper training and depression screening. Gatekeeper training involves "increasing awareness of warning signs within teachers, administrators, and other school personnel, and teaching referral skills" (Lieberman et al., 2008, pp. 1461). Furthermore, the program increases students' awareness of suicide utilizing a thirty-minute educational video to outline suicide warning signs, stress the significance of youth seeking adult assistance in dealing with suicidal ideation, and the importance of utilizing crisis hotlines (Lieberman et al., 2008).

Along with Gatekeeper training, the Signs of Suicide program provides a brief depression questionnaire in which the student is asked to complete and score. If the child's score falls in the clinically significant range for depression, the interpretation sheet encourages the youth to seek help immediately (Lieberman et al., 2008). Ultimately, the Signs of Suicide program seeks to assist youth in identifying the symptoms of depression and suicidality in themselves, their friends, or other students within the school.

Another suicide prevention program designed to screen youth at-risk for suicide is the CARE/CAST program. The CARE/CAST program is an acronym for **C**are, **A**ssess, **R**espond, **E**mpower/**C**oping and **S**upport **T**raining. The CARE/CAST program evaluates students' risk for committing suicide by having youth complete a computer assisted suicide assessment and counseling intervention. (Katz et al., 2013). The goals of the CARE program are to decrease suicidal behaviors and risk factors (Katz et al., 2013). Additionally, the CAST program is a prevention program that seeks of increase life skills and social support (Katz et al., 2013)

Finally, although the original intent of the Good Behavior Game was to create a classroom management approach through rewarding students who follow classroom rules, it has been shown effective in reducing suicidal ideation and suicide attempts in youth (Katz et al., 2013). In fact, the Good Behavior Game and Signs of Suicide Program are the only evidence-based programs that have been shown to reduced suicide attempts in youth. The Good Behavior Game is the only program shown to reduce suicidal ideation (Katz et al., 2013).

At the Tier 1 level, school psychologists are in an ideal position to educate and provide in-service trainings to educators on the warning signs of youth suicide along with the referral process for a child who may be experiencing suicidal ideation. Lieberman et al. (2008) writes that "teachers and other adults who have frequent interactions with adolescents can be extremely important in the prevention of suicide" (p. 1462). Thus, educators should be made aware that youth who engage in suicidal ideation often vocalize threats of committing suicide, reveal plans to commit suicide, attempted suicide in the past, appear depressed or irritated, exhibit sudden changes in behavior or personality, or give away prized possessions.

Furthermore, the school psychologist should collaborate with educators in dealing with suicidal youth as many difficult decisions have to be made at the administrative level. Hence, school psychologists should outline a plan with the school crisis team that involves roles and responsibilities of team members and general guidelines for staff to follow. The protocol should involve steps such as supervising the student and does not allow the student to be alone or leave the school. Additionally, the protocol should involve steps such as informing the youth of the actions to be taken as a result of finding out about their suicidal ideation, suicide-proofing the school environment, utilizing law enforcement when necessary, and preparing a plan for the youth to reenter the school when they are no longer a danger to themselves (Lieberman et al., 2008).

Tier II Intervention Efforts:

Tier 2 is designed for students who are at risk for suicidal behaviors due to having some identifiable risk factor such as a previous suicide attempt, history of depression, social isolation, or substance abuse (Miller, 2014). At the Tier 2 level, intervention efforts involve completing a suicide risk/threat assessment, mobilizing a support system, and group cognitive-behavioral therapy (Lieberman et al., 2008; Miller, 2014).

An instrument that may be useful in determining whether a youth is at-risk for committing suicide is the Columbia Suicide Severity Rating Scale (C-SSRS). The C-SSRS comes in a 6 question screener that is available for free and is designed to be used in a number of settings such as schools, hospitals, and agencies (C-SSRS, n. d.). In the assessing suicidal risk, the C-SSRS is a vital tool that may provide insight as to whether a youth is at-risk for committing suicide, but ultimately clinical judgement should be utilized.

When a youth has been identified as having risk factors for suicide, it is critical for the school psychologist and educators to identify and establish a support system for the child. Simply asking the child "who do you want to be here for you right now?" may provide the student with a sense of control over their fate during the difficult challenges that lay ahead (Lieberman et al, 2008). Overall, a student's support system may consist of individuals that the youth identifies with and feels close to such as family members, friends, teachers, coaches, and pastors. The primary role of mobilizing a support system is to socially engage the youth in conversation, activities, and healthy forms of coping in stressful situations.

In regards to group cognitive-behavior therapy, school-based CBT programs, such as the POD-Teams Depression Prevention Program, may assist youth in challenging and altering negative thoughts and irrational feelings that may be contributing to the youth's problems (Miller, 2014). Finally, at this Tier, the school may want to assist the child's caregivers in finding community resources and outside therapists that may further benefit the child in overcoming feelings of sadness, anxiety, or isolation. For example, the community may have depression or anxiety groups for youth or outside clinicians that will work with the school system in assisting the youth to overcome depression.

The Good Behavior Game and Signs of Suicide Program are the only evidence-based programs that have been shown to reduce suicide attempts in youth. The Good Behavior Game is the only program shown to reduce suicidal ideation (Katz et al., 2013).

Tier III Intervention Efforts:

Tier 3 intervention efforts revolve around responding to a referral that a student is potentially suicidal and involves further assessment of the student's risk for committing suicide. Informing and interviewing the parents about a child's suicidal ideation involves asking four questions. First, is the parent available? Second, is the parent cooperative? Third, what information does the parent have that might contribute to the assessment of risk? Fourth, what mental health insurance, if any, does the family have? (Lieberman et al., 2008). Additional assessment of the student's risk for committing suicide involves gathering information from staff members, teachers, and the student (Lieberman et al., 2008). School psychologists should be prepared with a set of questions to assesses the student's risk for completing suicide by asking questions such as "have you ever tried to kill yourself in the past?" or "do you have a plan in place to kill yourself?" Moreover, the school psychologist may want to ask the student's teachers and parents if they noticed a sudden change in the youth's behavior. Lastly, the school psychologist and school-based mental health practitioners should remove student access to any possible lethal weapons or medications and ensure that the child is supervised at all times (Miller, 2014).

In regards to locating outside assistance, the school psychologist should assist the family in locating community services to assist their child in overcoming his/her suicidal ideation by taking into account both their insurance and culture. For example, a student's family may feel more comfortable receiving treatment for their child through a religious leader in the community rather than through a counselor. Moreover, when collaborating with community agencies over a youth who is suicidal it is important that the school psychologist provide accurate assessment information that the parent may omit (Lieberman et al., 2008).

Finally, after a student has been assessed for risk and is receiving the appropriate mental health support, the school psychologist should follow up on the student's progress and act as a liaison between the home, school, and community resource environments (Lieberman et al., 2008). The school psychologist should work with other school and community-based mental health care practitioners and school administrators to devise a plan in helping the student re-enter the school when the child is prepared to return. At this Tier, more intensive 1:1 counseling may be needed. School psychologists are recommended to work extensively with outside clinicians on developing a plan that assists the child both inside and outside the school environment (Lieberman et al., 2008; Miller, 2014).

CLICK HERE TO PLAY SUICIDE PREVENTIONTION & INTERNENTION VIDEO

Figure 21 **Suicide Prevention and Intervention MTSS Flow Chart**

- ✓ **Educate staff, students, and parents on the warning signs of suicidal behavior through programs such as the Signs of Suicide, CARE/CAST, or other means**
- ✓ **Create warm, caring, supportive and welcoming school environment**
- ✓ **Universally screen all students for social-emotional concerns using the Behavior Intervention Monitoring System (BIMAS), Behavior and Emotional Screening System (BESS), Student Internalizing Behavior Screener (SIBS) etc.**
- ✓ **Examine screening results and identify at-risk youth**
- ✓ **Consult with parents and child if social-emotional concerns are present**
- ✓ **Suicide threat → Tier 3**

Student Does Not Show Risk Signs for Suicide

Student Shows Some Risk Signs for Suicide (sadness, isolation, past attempts)

- ✓ **Assess the student's risk for suicide using the Columbia Suicide Severity Rating Scale (C-SSRS), Slap Dirt Suicide Assessment, or other means. If child deemed at serious risk → Tier 3 and consult outside clinician**
- ✓ **Identify & mobilize a support system for at-risk child**
- ✓ **Ask the child "who do you want to be here right now?"**
- ✓ **United child with loved ones at home, in the community, and at school on a daily basis**
- ✓ **Utilize social skills and replacement behavior/cognition groups and CBT groups. Track student progress using C-RSS, BIMAS etc.**
- ✓ **Provide parents/caregiver community resources and outside clinicians who may further assist in addressing feelings of sadness, anxiety etc. (i.e. child depression group, anxiety group).**
- ✓ **Involve the child in activities and tasks that he/she likes. *Refer to Tier 3 if suicide threat.***

Student Does Not Show Risk for Suicide

Student Shows Risk Signs for Committing Suicide

- ✓ ***Do NOT leave child alone***
- ✓ **Refer to district suicide risk manual**
- ✓ **Remove access to all lethal means to commit suicide (access to guns, knives, keys, medications)**
- ✓ **Interview parents**
- ✓ **Identify and further access school and community resources**
- ✓ **Refer and coordinate efforts with outside clinician or hospital**

Work with outside clinician, administration, and parents to devise school re-entry plan when student is stable

Created by Gary Schaffer ©

Social Emotional & Suicide Interventions & Resources

#'s of Pictures Correspond to Resource Links on the Next Page

1) Identifying ED

Identifying Emotional Disturbance:

Guidance for School Psychologists

Stephen E. Brock, PhD, NCSP, LEP
Professor & School Psychology Program Coordinator;
California State University, Sacramento

National Association of School
Psychologists
2015 Summer Conference
Atlantic City, New Jersey

July 22, 2015

2) BIMAS

3) DESSA Screener

DESSA
DEVEREUX STUDENT
STRENGTHS ASSESSMENT
K-8TH GRADE

A MEASURE OF
SOCIAL-EMOTIONAL
COMPETENCIES OF
CHILDREN IN
KINDERGARTEN
THROUGH EIGHTH GRADE

Paul A. LeBuffe, Valerie B. Shapiro, & Jack A. Naglieri

4) SIBSS

Student Internalizing Behavior Screening Scale (SIBSS)

Directions: Please rate each student on each behavior using the following scale:
(0=Never, 1=Rarely, 2=Occasionally, 3=Frequently)

Student Name	Nervous or fearful	Bullied by peers	Spends time alone	Disinterested	Withdrawn	Seems sad or unhappy	Complains about being sick or hurt

5) Youth Depression Treatment and Prevention Programs

Intervention title	Purpose
Adolescent Coping With Depression Course (CWD-A)	Group Treatment
Group for Parents of Depressed Youth	Companion to youth Treatment
Coping with Stress Course (CWS)	Group Prevention
Brief Individual CBT Program	Individual Treatment
POD-TEAMS Depression prevention program	Group Prevention

6) CBITS for Trauma

Cognitive Behavioral Intervention for Trauma in Schools

Home | Learn More | About Us | Success Stories | News | School Crises

School Crises

Please click here for more information about helping students through school crises.

CBITS At-a-Glance

7) SSET for Trauma

Support for Students Exposed to Trauma

Support for Students Exposed to Trauma (SSET) is an evidence-based intervention focused on managing the distress that results from exposure to trauma. Designed to be implemented by teachers or school counselors with groups or 8-10 students, SSET is a 10-lesson curriculum. The program includes skill-building techniques to reduce current problems with anxiety, worry, and depressed mood and to help students deal with real-life problems and stressors. The SSET program encourages students to draw or write about their traumatic experiences in order to process their emotions.

Particularly useful in situations where there is no or limited support from mental-health clinicians, SSET provides teachers with the tools and confidence to support trauma-exposed students, whether the trauma is environmental and chronic or is related to a single traumatic event.

Training to implement the SSET program is available online or through in-person training. Visit www.ssetprogram.org for more information.

8) Principal's Research Review

Principal's
Research Review

Supporting the Principal's Data-Informed Decisions
ISSN-1558-5948   VOL. 8, ISSUE 6   NOVEMBER 2013

The Role of Schools in Supporting Traumatized Students

By Eric Rossen and Katherine Cowan

Childhood trauma is among the most relevant and significant psychosocial factors affecting education today (Blaustein, 2013). The effects of those trauma are far reaching, with the potential to influence students, families, educators, and the overall school culture. Exposure to adverse experiences and childhood trauma poses a significant risk to student learning and mental health and is far more pervasive than previously thought. Whether the trauma is the result of chronic adverse experiences (e.g., neglect) or an acute crisis event (e.g., a nat-

Schools are well-suited to offer an engaging presence of trained, caring, stable adults, a learning environment that can naturally support and develop resilience and coping skills, and partnerships with families and community providers to help provide comprehensive supports.

Addressing trauma and its related issues is essential to the mission and purpose of schools: learning. Traumatized students are often focused on survival, which hampers their ability to learn, socialize, and develop the skills needed to thrive. Failure to provide

Traumatized students are often focused on survival, which hampers their ability to learn, socialize, and develop the skills needed to thrive.

9) Suicide Risk Scale

COLUMBIA-SUICIDE SEVERITY RATING SCALE (C-SSRS)

ABOUT THE C-SSRS | PUBLIC HEALTH | RESEARCH | MEDIA/PRESS | CONTACT

...t ask.

...ause you can save a life.

Central to effectively implementing MTSS across the academic, behavioral, and social-emotional domains is the continued reallocation of roles for school psychologists. School psychologists reprising their role as "special education gatekeeper" and "tester" must be replaced by more diverse responsibilities that promote preventative practices under an MTSS model. Therefore, schools should take advantage of school psychologists' unique skillsets in the areas of intervention design/implementation, progress monitoring, consultation, counseling, crisis prevention, and program research. Still, many school psychologists remain in their traditional roles. A study conducted by Brown, Holcombe, Bolen, and Thomson (2006) revealed that school psychologists spend up to two-thirds of their time on assessment activities related to special education. However, school psychologists expressed wanting to spend less time in assessment and multidisciplinary team meetings and more time delivering and implementing interventions (Brown et al., 2006).

With MTSS continuing to gain momentum in schools, a broadening of roles for school psychologists appears to be underway. In 2010, Sullivan and Long found that 87.5% of school psychologists reported being directly involved in the implementation of Response to Intervention. Despite school psychologists' roles expanding, many professionals in the field continue to engage in the "traditionalistic" practices of conducting psycho-educational evaluations and writing reports in addition to their responsibilities under an MTSS model (Sullivan & Long, 2010).

In order to successfully embrace and sustain MTSS, school psychologists must be utilized in ways that exploit their training under such models in lieu of reenacting their former more restrictive roles. There is growing recognition that school psychologists are uniquely trained in the design, delivery, and implementation of MTSS and are qualified mental health providers (Sullivan & Long, 2010; National Association of School Psychologists, 2016). To address the expanding role of school psychologists and promote childhood mental health, the National Association of School Psychologists recommends a ratio of 1 school psychologist per 500 to 700 students (Skalski et al., 2015). However, the ratio of students to school psychologists may be reduced further for high needs schools in impoverished or rural areas. In these cases, the ratio to best address student needs may be as little as 1 school psychologist for every 200 to 400 students.

In order for school districts to successfully implement MTSS, school administrators need to closely examine the current roles of their school-based mental health practitioners and determine whether these professionals are being utilized in a manner that best supports preventative practices. For example, school psychologists who are spending a large portion of their day engaged in psycho-educational assessment and report writing will have less time to dedicate to preventative practices such as intervention design and implementation, counseling, and teacher consultation. The less time school psychologists and school-based mental health practitioners spend on embracing preventative practices under MTSS, the more they are likely to be engaging in a reactionary "wait-to-fail" model. Therefore, it is critical that school districts maintain adequate school-based mental health staffing to best place students, teachers, and administrators in an optimum position to support successful learning environments.

Although school psychologists are primarily restricted to providing their services in school settings in NYS, the "school" in school psychology represents the type of psychology practiced and not the specific location. Therefore, in addition to providing vital academic, behavioral, and social-emotional supports in schools, expansion of school psychology services outside the typical school day and into the community may provide much needed mental and behavioral health services to children and their families. Outside the school day, school psychologists may provide children educationally related counseling for test anxiety, facilitate a social skills group for students with autism, conduct behavior management sessions, develop and consult over educational programs, or complete psycho-educational assessments.

With shortages of childhood mental health practitioners across NYS and the nation, expansion of school psychology services is greatly needed to provide children behavioral, social, and emotional supports. Finally, although standardized psycho-educational assessments have their place in school psychology practice, there continued overuse is unwarranted and unnecessary as each allocates significant time and resources away from school psychologists being actively involved designing, implementing, and monitoring MTSS implementation. Under an MTSS model, school psychologists are actively involved with all children and not only those most in need of their services. Lastly, school districts should seek to provide school psychologists and school-based mental health practitioners' in-service trainings to keep them up-to-date on their roles and practices under MTSS.

CLICK HERE TO PLAY
RESOURCE ALLOCATION VIDEO

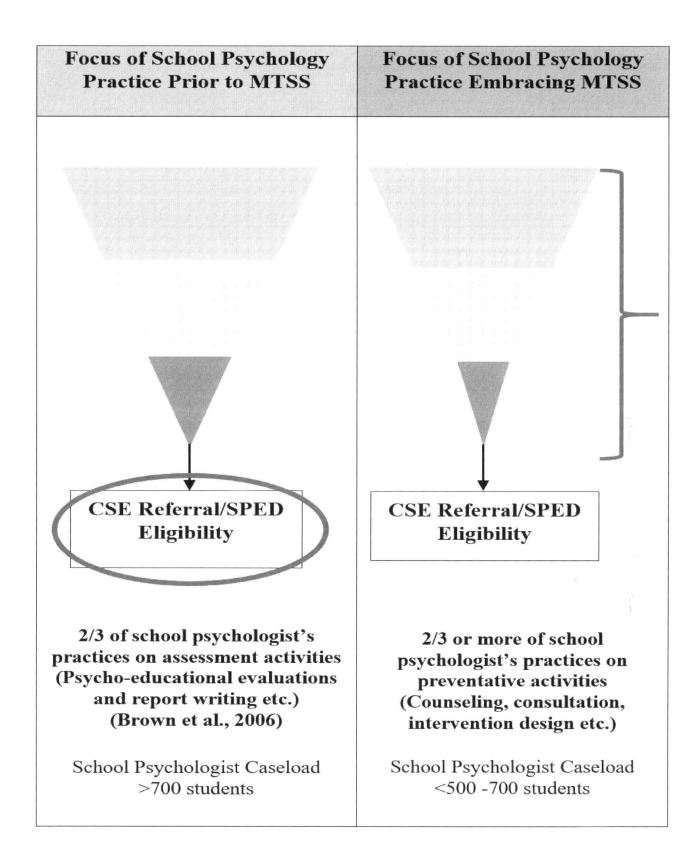

Focus of School Psychology Practice Prior to MTSS	Focus of School Psychology Practice Embracing MTSS
CSE Referral/SPED Eligibility	CSE Referral/SPED Eligibility
2/3 of school psychologist's practices on assessment activities (Psycho-educational evaluations and report writing etc.) (Brown et al., 2006)	**2/3 or more of school psychologist's practices on preventative activities (Counseling, consultation, intervention design etc.)**
School Psychologist Caseload >700 students	School Psychologist Caseload <500 -700 students

NASP PPRACTICE MODEL FOR COMPREHENSIVE AND
INTEGRATIVE SCHOOL PSYCHOLOGICAL SERVICES

Final Thoughts

Multi-tiered systems of support are an evidence-based framework for comprehensively coordinating and delivering interventions to students across the academic, behavioral, and social-emotional domains (National Association of School Psychologists, 2016). MTSS is based on preventative, as opposed to reactionary practices in ensuring that all students have the best opportunity to learn and succeed in school and in life. The defining attribute of MTSS is that schools do not wait for students to experience significant difficulties before intervention and support is offered. Instead, schools embracing MTSS operate under the premise of preventing students from experiencing difficulty and should students begin to struggle offering prescribed programs to best remediate area(s) of concern. For those districts that recognize the importance of MTSS, resources will be allocated more effectively, education funds will be replete, special education rates will decline considerably, and all children will be provided a better opportunity than ever to succeed in the educational environment through early intervention services before having to simply "wait to fail."

A testament to any sound comprehensive MTSS model is its ability to transcend school districts and have a lasting positive effect on the surrounding community. Critical to MTSS having a considerable effect on the community, and society as a whole, is for students to be offered and provided comprehensive mental health services beyond the typical school day. Consequently, it is vital that school-based mental health practitioners expand their roles to effectively meet the needs of children at-risk or presenting with mental health concerns. Additionally, schools must fully embrace their role as "de facto" mental health centers that children, parents, and families turn to because many place inherent trust and security in educators. For far too long, teachers and parents have realized that a child's difficulties do not simply stop at the school doorstep. Embracing MTSS at the school and community level offers the best opportunity in helping children succeed.

CLICK HERE TO PLAY FINAL THOUGHTS VIDEO

To learn more about preventative practice, provide a book review, or report broken links, please visit:
http://geschaffer.wixsite.com/nutsandbolts

Video Presenter Contacts and Biographies

Contact Information for Future Consults (Biographies on Next Page):

- *Gary Schaffer; Author: geschaffer@gmail.com*

- *Dr. Lisa Kilanowski; Editor: lak@niagara.edu*

- *Dr. Laura Spencely: laura.spenceley@oswego.edu*

- *Dr. John Garruto: jgarruto@verizon.net*

- *Mrs. Dawn Catucci: catdawn1@aol.com*

- *Dr. Don Merriman: drmerriman@ymail.com*

- *Dr. James McDougal: james.mcdougal@oswego.edu*

- *Mrs. Kelly Caci: legislative@nyasp.org*

- *Dr. Williams-Ceeatow: Stacy.williams@marist.edu*

To learn more about preventative practice, provide a book review, or report broken links, please visit:

http://geschaffer.wixsite.com/nutsandbolts

Gary Schaffer; Author
M. S./C.A.S. School Psychology
B. A. Special Education & English
NYS OPWDD & OMH School Psychologist
Frontier CSD & ECMC School Psychologist

Gary Schaffer is a School Psychologist and author of the book *Nuts & Bolts: Multi-Tiered Systems of Support: A Basic Guide to Implementing Preventative Practice in Our Schools and Community.* Gary currently works for the NYS Office of People with Developmental Disabilities and Frontier Central School District. Additionally, he provides assessment services Erie County Medical Center and is an Adjunct Professor of School Psychology at Niagara University. He has previously been employed by the NYS Office of Mental Health, Lansing School District, and Dysart Unified School District.

Gary received his B.A. degree in Special Education and English and M.S./C.A.S. degree in School Psychology from Niagara University in Niagara University, NY. He is a past recipient of the New York Association of School Psychologists' (NYASP) Ted Bernstein Award and currently serves on the NYASP Board. In June, 2015, Gary met with national House and Senate members in Washington, DC to support the inclusion of childhood mental health and Multi-Tiered Systems of Support in the Every Student Succeeds Act (ESSA).

He has previously published for the Encyclopedia of Child Behavior and Development, Journal of Post-Secondary Education and Disability, and the New York School Psychologist. At present, Gary is leading a national study analyzing motivational factors and compensatory strategies of high school, post-secondary, and college alumni with High Functioning Autism. His research interests include Multi-Tiered Systems of Support, post-secondary transition for students with disabilities, school and community-based mental health, ADHD, and developmental disabilities.

Gary can be reached for consultation and presentations at geschaffer@gmail.com

Dr. Lisa Kilanowski; Editor
D. Ed School Psychology
Assoc. Professor of School Psychology; Niagara University
Trainers of School Psychologists-NY President

Dr. Lisa Kilanowski is an associate professor of school psychology at Niagara University and school psychology program director. Along with being program director at Niagara University, Dr. Kilanowski is a New York Association of School Psychologists Board Member and President for the Trainers of School Psychologists-NY, which represents all 27 graduate programs of School Psychology in NYS.

Dr. Kilanowski's primary research interests include response to intervention, reading disabilities, assessment and intervention in reading, math, and written expression, school reform and systems change, leadership in the profession of school psychology, and advanced integration of neuropsychological principles and RtI data in the assessment of learning disabilities in K-12 environments.

Dr. Kilanowski routinely provides extensive district consultation, policy writing assistance, and professional development regarding the implementation of K-12 RtI models across NYS, in addition to presenting on the subject nationally. Since 2008, Dr. Kilanowski has trained over 2,700 school district and building leaders, school psychologists, and teachers via the provision of 97 workshops dedicated to various aspects of RtI implementation

Dr. Kilanowski has served as a workshop provider for the Erie County Bar Association Committee for the Disabled, providing professional development to attorneys who work with individuals with disabilities.

Dr. Kilanowski can be reached for consultation and presentations at *lak@niagara.edu*

Dr. Andrew Shanock; Editor
School Psychology Professor St. Rose University
NYASP Past President

Dr. Andrew Shanock has been teaching at The College of Saint Rose since 2005 and is the past president of the New York Association of School Psychologists. He specializes in cognitive and academic assessment. He brings to the classroom his years of experience as a school psychologist in public, parochial, and charter schools within urban, suburban, and rural districts. Dr. Shanock's primary interest is the continued development and understanding of contemporary assessment techniques including the Cattell-Horn-Carroll (CHC) Cross Battery and Response to Intervention. He promotes an awareness of what cognitive abilities tests actually measure and how cultural and linguistic loadings can impact performance and interpretation. He is currently consulting with several districts in the Capital Region on the creation and implementation of Response to Intervention policies and procedures as well as the development of Instructional Support Teams.

Dr. John Garruto
Oswego City School District; School Psychologist
SUNY Oswego Adjunct Professor
NYASP President-Elect

Dr. John Garruto has worked as a school psychologist in Central New York for nearly 20 years. Additionally, he has taught college courses in cognitive assessment, ethics, and educationally disabling conditions. He is currently the President-Elect of the New York Association of School Psychologists, after having served as Research Chair for five years. Dr. Garruto also serves as an at-large member of the Ethics and Professional Practices Committee of the National Association of School Psychologists. He has authored or co-authored various chapters and books. His most recent publication, along with Dr. Fredrick Schrank and Dr. Scott Decker is the Essentials of WJ-IV Cognitive Abilities Assessment. Dr. Garruto's primary interests relate to the assessment for learning disabilities, neuropsychology, and professional practice. *He can be reached for consult at: jgarruto@verizon.net*

Dr. John Kelly
Commack School District; School Psychologist
NASP President
NYASP Legislative Co-Chair

Dr. John Kelly is a school psychologist in the Commack School District and an Adjunct Professor at St. John's University in the School Psychology program. He earned his Ph.D. in Clinical and School Psychology from Hofstra University. Dr. Kelly has studied, published, and presented at numerous national and international conferences on topics that include mental and behavioral health services for children, advocacy training for school psychologists, leadership development, violence and bullying prevention, and suicide awareness.

Dr. Kelly is on the Executive Board of the New York Association of School Psychologists (NYASP) and serves on the Board of Directors of the National Association of School Psychologists (NASP). He is the President of NASP. Dr. Kelly has received numerous state and national awards, including the NYS School Practitioner of the Year in 2001 and the NASP School Psychologist of the Year in 2003.

Dr. Laura Spencely
Associate Professor SUNY Oswego

Dr. Laura Spencely is an assistance professor of counseling and psychological services at SUNY Oswego. Dr. Spencely currently serves on the NYASP Board in the capacity of student liaison. In addition to her duties at SUNY Oswego, Dr. Spencely works as a per diem school psychologist for the Fulton School District.

Dr. Spencely obtained her Ph.D. in School Psychology from Syracuse University and has a master's in Clinical Psychology from Ball State University. She has presented internationally on selecting assessment tools to inform psycho-educational decision-making and improving the accuracy of psycho-educational evaluations. *Dr. Spencely can be reached for consultation at: laura.spenceley@oswego.edu*

Dr. James McDougal
Co-Author: BIMAS & BIMAS-2
Director of School Psychology
SUNY Oswego

Dr. James McDougal has over two decades of experience as a practicing school psychologist in an urban context and has conducted over 300 training seminars in the areas of academic and behavioral assessment/intervention. He is highly familiar with Response-to-Intervention (RTI) models and the NYSED Diagnostic Tool for School and District Effectiveness. Dr. McDougal is the Director of the School Psychology Program at the State University of New York at Oswego. A state-approved PBIS trainer, he is also co-author of the Behavior Intervention Monitoring and Assessment System, used to screen and monitor progress of students with social-emotional and behavioral difficulties. He is the former Mental Health Coordinator for the Syracuse City School District. Dr. McDougal also published 2 books and over 30 peer-reviewed articles. He holds a PhD degree from SUNY Albany. *He can be reached for consult at: james.mcdougal@oswego.edu*

Dawn Catucci
M.S., Ed, PD, LMHC
Ardsley School District; School Psychologist

Dawn Catucci is currently a school psychologist at Ardsley High School and has been a school psychologist for 20 years. Mrs. Catucci is also a part-time Dialectical Behavior Therapy (DBT) School Consultant Trainer for Cognitive Behavioral Consultants and maintains a private practice in Pleasantville, NY. Mrs. Catucci is a NYS Certified School Psychologist and a NYS Licensed Mental Health Counselor (LMHC). She is extensively trained in dialectical behavior therapy and in cognitive behavior therapy (CBT). In 2008, Mrs. Catucci and her colleagues at Ardsley High School were one of the first schools to implement comprehensive DBT in a school setting and are now implementing CBT in a school setting as well. She is highly interested in dissemination of evidenced based practice for counseling practices in schools. Mrs. Catucci has also facilitated CBT and DBT trainings for several other school districts and school psychologists across Westchester County. Ms. Catucci has co-presented at a state conference and a local NASP chapter workshop on Utilizing Comprehensive CBT in a School Setting. Mrs. Catucci is a New York Association School Psychologist Board Member, serving on multiple conference committees' and as the Chapter L Alt Representative since 2009. *She can be reached for consult at: catdawn1@aol.com*

Dr. Don Merriman
School Psychologist; North Salem School District

Dr. Don Merriman, has been a practicing school psychologist since 2003 and is currently employed by the North Salem School District. He also maintains a private practice with offices in Mahopac and Pleasantville, New York. Additionally, Dr. Merriman is a NYASP Board Member, serving as the 2017 Conference Co-Chair. Dr. Merriman has completed extensive training in Cognitive Behavior Therapy (CBT) at the Beck Institute. He obtained his Ph.d in the Educational Psychology, School Psychology Specialization from the Graduate Center of the City of New York and additionally holds his Master's of Science in Education. Dr. Marriman and his colleague, Katia Castelli, have been instrumental in bringing CBT to the North Salem School District, with the goal of establishing a continuum of support in grades K-12. *He can be reached for consult at: drmerriman@ymail.com*

Kelly Caci
School Psychologist
Newburgh Enlarged City School District
NYASP Legislative Co-Chair

Kelly Caci is a NYS school psychologist employed by the Newburgh Enlarged City School District in in New Windsor, NY. She is also a past president of the New York Association of School Psychologists and current legislative chair. While president of NYASP, Kelly initiated a campaign to highlight effective elements of school safety planning and the provision of mental health services in the schools. She remains a strong proponent of the NYS School Psychologist Licensure Bill and has conducted interviews with the ChildMind Institute regarding the practice of school psychology. *She can be reached for consult at: legislative@nyasp.org*

Dr. Stacy A. S. Williams, PhD, NCSP
Assistant Professor of Psychology
Trainers of School Psychologists (TSP) Membership Coordinator

Stacy A. S. Williams, Ph.D., NCSP is an Assistant Professor at Marist College, Licensed Psychologist and Certified School Psychologist in New York State. In the past, she directed the field-training program at University at Albany. Her years of working with groups of K-12 at-risk learners in both urban and rural communities have provided her with clear insights into the frustrations, challenges and joys of working as a school psychologist with limited resources. She has consulted with Instructional Support Teams (IST) (NY & CT), Behavior Specialists at the state level (NY), and rural educators in Jamaica. Her research focuses on effective consultation practices with teachers. *She can be reached for consult at: Stacy.williams@marist.edu*

References

American Institute for Research (n. d.). *Good behavior game.* Washington, DC: Author Retrieved

from http://www.air.org/topic/p-12-education-and-social-development/good-behavior-

game

Ardoin, S. P., & Christ T. J. (2009). Curriculum-based measurement of oral reading: Standard

errors associated with progress monitoring outcomes from DIBELS, AIMSweb, and an

experimental passage set. *School Psychology Review 38*(2), 266 – 283. Retrieved from

www.cehd.umn.edu/edpsych/faip-r/documents/standarderrorsprogressmonitoring.pdf.

Army Medicine (Photographer). (2014, January 16). *Teacher helping pupils studying at desks in*

classroom [digital image]. Retrieved from https://www.flickr.com/photos/armymedicine

/13584535514/

Attendance Works & Everyone Graduates (2016). *Preventing missed opportunity: Taking*

collective action to confront chronic absence. Retrieved from http://www.attendance

works.org/research/preventing-missed-opportunity/

Averill, O. H., & Rinaldi, C. (2011). Multi-tier system of supports. *District Administration 47*(8),

91 – 95. Retrieved from https://www.researchgate.net/profile/Claudia_Rinaldi/

publication/257943817_Multitier_System_of_Supports_A_Description_of_RTI_and_

PBIS_Models_for_District_Administrators/links/0046352669d913a09d000000.pdf

Balfanz, R., & Byrnes, V. (2012). *Chronic Absenteeism: Summarizing what we know from*

nationally available data. Baltimore, MD: Johns Hopkins University Center for Social

Organization of Schools. Retrieved from: content/uploads/2012/05http://new.every1

graduates.org/wpFINALChronic/AbsenteeismReport_May16.pdf

BASC-3: Behavior and emotional screening system (BESS). (n. d.). Retrieved from

http://www.pearsonclinical.com/education/products/100001482/basc3-behavioral-and-

emotional-screeningsystem--basc-3-bess.html

Beck Youth Inventories: Second Edition. (n. d.). Retrieved from http://www.pearsonclinical.com
/psychology/products/100000153/beck-youth-inventories-second-edition-byi-ii.html

Behavior intervention monitoring assessment system (BIMAS). (n. d.). Retrieved from
http://www.mhs.com/product.aspx?gr=edu&id=overview&prod=bimas

Brown, M. B., Holcombe, D. C., Bolen, L. M., & Thomsom, W. S. (2006). Role function and job
satisfaction of school psychologists practicing in an expanded role model.
Psychological Reports, 98(2), 486 – 496. doi: 10.2466/pr0.98.2

Canter, A., Klotz, M. B., & Cowan, K. (2008). Response to intervention: The future for secondary
schools. *Principal Leadership, 8*(6), 12 – 15. Retrieved from
https://www.nasponline.org
/Documents/Resources20and%20Publications/Handouts/Families%20and%20Educator
s/RTI%20Part%201-NASSP%20February%2008.pdf

Center for Mental Health Services, Substance Abuse and Mental Health Services Administration
(SAMHSA) (2012). *Preventing suicide: A toolkit for high schools* (HHS Publication
No. 02-2650). Retrieved from http://store.samhsa.gov/product/Preventing-Suicide-A-
Toolkit-for-High-Schools/SMA12-4669

Children's depression inventory 2 (CDI 2). (n. d.). Retrieved from http://www.mhs.com/product.
aspx?gr=edu&id=overview&prod=cdi2

Christ, T. J., Zopluoglu, C., Monaghen, B. D., & Van Norman, E. R. (2013). Curriculum-based
measurement of oral reading: Multi-study evaluation of schedule, duration, and dataset
quality on progress monitoring outcomes. *Journal of School Psychology, 51*(1), 19 –
57. doi: 10.1016/j.jsp.2012.11.001

Chronic Absence (n. d.). Retrieved from http://gradelevelreading.net/our-work/chronic-absence

The Devereux Student Strengths Assessment (n. d.). Retrieved from http://www.centerforresilient

children.org/school-age/assessments-resources/the-devereux-student-strengths-

assessment-mini-dessa-mini-kit/

Cognitive behavioral intervention in schools (CBITS) (n. d.). Retrieved from https://cbitsprogram

.org/

Council on School Health (2013). Out of school suspension and expulsion. *Pediatrics, 131*(3),

999 – 1007. doi: 10.1542/peds.2012-3932

Daly, B. P., Nicholls, E., Aggarwal, R., & Sander, M. (2014). Promoting social competence and

reducing behavior problems in at-risk students: Implementation and efficacy of

universal and selective prevention programs in schools. In Weist, M., Lever, N.,

Bradshaw, C., & Owens (Eds.), *Handbook of school mental health: Research,*

training, practice, and policy (2nd ed.) (pp. 131 – 144). New York, NY: Springer

Drummond, R. (1993). The student risk screening scale (SRSS). Grants Pass, OR: Josephine

County Mental Health Program.

Fiorillo, J. & Long, J. (2012, July). Dialectical behavior therapy skills groups in schools: A

review of empirical findings. *From Science to Practice.* Retrieved from:

http://www.apadivisions.org/ division-16/publications/newsletters/science

/2012/07/empirical-findings.aspx

Forness, S., & Knitzer, J. (1992). A new proposed definition and terminology to replace "serious

emotional disturbance" in Individuals with Disabilities Education Act. *School*

Psychology Review, 21(1), 12-20.

Fuchs, L.S., & Deno, S.L. (1991). Paradigmatic distinctions between instructionally relevant

measurement models. *Exceptional Children, 57*(6), 488–500.

Frey, A. J., Lingo, A. S., & Nelson, C. M. (2010). Implementing positive behavior support in

elementary schools. In M. R. Shinn & H. M. Walker (Eds.), *Interventions for achievement and behavior problems in a three-tier model including RTI* (pp. 397 –

433). Washington, DC: National Association of School Psychologists.

GETSCHOOLED (2012). *Skipping to Nowhere.* Retrieved from

http://www.attendanceworks.org/

wordpress/wp-content/uploads/2013/10/Skipping-to-Nowhere-August-2012.pdf

Gillham, J., Reivich, K., & Seligman, M. E.P. (n. d.). The penn resiliency program. Retrieved

from http://www.positivepsychology.org/research/resilience-children

Gresham, F. M. (2005). Response to Intervention: An alternative means of identifying students

as emotionally disturbed. *Education and Treatment of Children, 28*(4), 328 – 344.

Retrieved from http://www.pent.ca.gov/pos/rti/rtialternativemeans_gresham.pdf

Gresham, F. M. (2007). Response to Intervention and Emotional Behavioral Disorders: Best

practices in assessment for intervention. *Assessment for Effective Intervention, 32*(4),

214 – 222. doi: 10.1177/15345084070320040301

Gresham, F. M., Reschly, D., & Shinn, M. R. (2010). RTI as a driving force in educational

improvement: Historical legal, research, and practice perspectives. In M. R. Shinn &

H. M. Walker (Eds.), *Interventions for achievement and behavior problems in a*

three-tier model, including RTI (pp. 47 – 78). Bethesda, MD: National Association of

School Psychologists.

Individuals With Disabilities Education Act, 20 U.S.C. § 1400 (2004).

Joyce-Beau, D., & Sulkowski, M. L., *Cognitive behavior therapy in k-12 school settings: A*

practitioner's toolkit. (2015). New York, NY: Springer.

Juszczak L., Melinkovich P., & Kaplan, D. (2003). Use of health and mental health services by

adolescents across multiple delivery sites. *Journal of Adolescent Health*, *32*(6 Suppl.),

108 – 118. doi:10.1016/S1054139X(03)00073-9

Katz, C., Bolton, S-L., Katz, L. Y., Isaak, C., Tilson-Jones, T., Sareen, J., & Cree, S. (2013). A
systematic review of school-based suicide prevention programs. *Depression and
Anxiety, 30*, 1030 – 1045. doi: 10.1002/da.22114

Kilanowski, L. (2010a). *Response to intervention: Essentials of implementation. Unpublished
manuscript*, Department of School Psychology, Niagara University, Niagara
University, United States of America.

Kilanowski, L. (2010b). *AIMSweb benchmarking and progress monitoring: An introduction*
Unpublished manuscript, Department of School Psychology, Niagara University,
Niagara University, United States of America.

LeBuffe, P. A. Shapiro, V. & Naglieri, J. A. (2008). *Devereux Student Strength Assessment*.
Cerritos, CA: Apperson.

Lieberman, R., Poland, S., & Cassel, R. (2008). Best practices in suicide intervention. In A.
Thomas & J. Grimes (Eds.), *Best practices in school psychology V* (pp. 1457 – 1472).
Bethesda, MD: National Association of School Psychologists.

Lever, N., Stephen, S., Castle M., Bernstein, L., Conners, E, Sharma, R., & Blizzard, A. (2015).
Community-Partnered School Behavioral Health: State of the Field in Maryland.
Baltimore, MD: Center for School Mental Health. Retrieved from
http://csmhumaryland
.edu/media/SOM/Microsites/CSMH/docs/Resources/Briefs/FINALCP.SBHReport3.5
.15_2.pdf

Livanis, A., Mulligan, C.A., Florin, D., & Mougrabi, R. (2012). Incorporating cognitive
behavior therapy in a school-wide positive behavioral support system: Promoting
good mental health in all children. In Mennuti, R. B., Christner, R.W., & Freeman, A.
(Eds.) *Cognitive-Behavioral Interventions in Educational Settings: A Handbook for
Practice* (2nd ed.). (683 – 720). New York: Routlege-Taylor & Francis Group.

Luiselli, J. K. & Diament, C. (2014). *Behavior psychology in the schools: Innovations in evaluation, support, and consultation*. New York, NY: Routledge

Macklem, G. L (2011). Evidence-based tier 1, tier 2, and tier 3 mental health interventions in schools. In *Evidence-based school mental health services: Affect education, emotion regulation training, and cognitive behavioral therapy* (pp. 19 - 37). Retrieved from http://www.springer.com/cda/content/document/cda_downloaddocument/9781441979 063-c1.pdf?SGWID=0-0-45- 1054638-p174060183

Mazza, J. J., & Reynolds, W. M. (2008). School-wide approaches to prevention of and treatment for depression and suicidal behaviors. In B. Doll & J. A. Cummings (Eds.). *Transforming school mental health services* (pp. 213 – 241). Thousand Oaks, CA: Corwin.

McDougal, J. L., Bardos, A. N., Meier, S. T. (n. d.). *BIMAS: Behavior Intervention Monitoring Assessment System* [Powerpoint slides]. Retrieved from https://masp.wildapricot.org/resourcesDocuments/2a%20%20Introducing%20the%20 BIMAS%20%20(handout%20in%20PDF).pdf

Mennuti, R. B., Christner, R. W., & Freeman, A. (2012). *Cognitive-behavioral interventions in educational settings: A handbook for practice* (2nd ed.). New York, NY: Taylor & Francis Group, LLC.

Mennuti, R. B., & Christner, R. W. (2012). An introduction to cognitive behavior therapy with youth. In R. B. Mennuti, R. W., Christner, & A. Freeman (Eds.), *Cognitive-behavioral interventions in educational settings: A handbook for practice* (2nd ed.) (pp. 3 – 23). New York, NY: Taylor & Francis

Merrell, K. W., & Walker, H. M. (2004). Deconstructing a definition: Social maladjustment versus emotional disturbance and moving the EBD field forward. *Psychology in the Schools, 41*(8), 899 – 909. doi: 10.1002/pits.20046

Miller, D. N. (2014). Levels of responsibility in school-based suicide prevention: Legal

    requirements, ethical duties, and best practices. *International Journal of Behavioral*

    Consultation and Therapy 9(3), 15 – 18.

Naglieri, J. A. (2011).The discrepancy/consistency approach to SLD identification using the

    PASS theory. In D. P. Flanagan & V. C. Alfonso (Eds.), Essentials of specific learning

    disability identification (pp. 145–172). Hoboken, NJ: Wiley.

Naglieri, J. A., LeBuffe, P. A., &Shapiro, V. (2010). *Devereux Student Strength Assessment –*

    mini. Cerritos, CA: Apperson.

Naglieri, J. A. & Otero, T. M. (2017) Essentials of CAS2 Assessment. New York: Wiley

    National Alliance on Mental Illness. (n. d.). *Mental health by the numbers.* Arlington,

    VA: Author Retrieved from https://www.nami.org/Learn-More/Mental-Health-By-the-

    Numbers

National Association of School Psychologists. (2016). *Leveraging essential school practices,*

    ESSA, MTSS, and the NASP practice model: A crosswalk to help every school and

    student succeed. [Policy brief]. Bethesda, MD: Author.

National Association of School Psychologists. (2005). *NASP position statement on students with*

    emotional and behavioral disorders. Bethesda, MD: Author. Retrieved from

    http://www4.smsd.org/kathygaskey/docsdoc-11786.pdf

National Association of School Psychologists. (2015). *School psychologists: Qualified health*

    professionals providing child and adolescent mental and behavioral health services

    [White paper]. Bethesda, MD: Author.

New York State Department of Health. (2011). *Suicide prevention, children ages 10 to 19 years.*

    Albany, NY: Author. Retrieved from https://www.health.ny.gov/prevention/injury_

    _prevention/children/fact_sheets/10-19_years/suicide_prevention_10-19_years.htm

New York State Office of Mental Health (2014). *The licensed mental health workforce in NYS: Size and geographic distribution—August, 2014.* Albany, NY: Author. Retrieved from https://www.omh. ny.gov/omhweb/special-projects/dsrip/docs/professional-shortage.pdf

New York State Office of Professions (2017). *License statistics.* Albany, NY: Author. Retrieved from http://www.op.nysed.gov/prof/psych/psychcounts.htm

Playingwithbrushes (Image Creator). (2006, November 6). Dog cute [digital image]. Retrieved from https://www.flickr.com/photos/playingwithpsp/290692791

Scharf, M. A., Alpert-Gillis, L. J., Wyman, P. A., White, A. M., Cerulli, C., Nichols-Hadeed, C.,…Wilson, J. (2015). *Promoting children's behavioral health: Examining needs, resources, and implementation of best-practices for children and youth in the Greater Rochester Area of New York State.* Rochester, NY: Greater Rochester Health Foundation. Retrieved from http://www.thegrhf.org/wp-content/uploads/Crisis-in-Care-Report-2016.pdf

Shapiro, E. S. (2013). Commentary on progress monitoring with CBM-R and decision making: Problems found and looking for solutions. *Journal of School Psychology 51*(1), 59 – 66. doi: 10.1016/j.jsp.2012.11.003

Shapiro, E.S., & Gebhardt, S. N. (2012). Comparing computer-adaptive and curriculum-based measurement methods of assessment. *School Psychology Review, 41*(3), 295 – 305. doi: 10.1016/j.jsp.2012.11.003

Shelly (Image Creator). (2014). *White dog* [digital image]. Retrieved from https://www. sketchport.com/drawing/6619249212653568/white-dog

Shinn, M. R. (2007). Identifying students at risk, monitoring performance, and determining eligibility within RTI; Research on educational need and benefit from academic intervention. *School Psychology Review, 36*(4), 601 – 617.

Shinn, M. R. (2010). Building a scientifically based data system for progress monitoring and universal screening across three tiers including RTI using Curriculum-Based Measurement. In M. R. Shinn & H. M. Walker (Eds.), *Interventions for achievement and behavior problems in a three-tier model, including rti* (pp. 259 – 292). Bethesda, MD: National Association of School Psychologists.

Shinn, M. R., & Walker, H. M. (2010). *Interventions for achievement and behavior problems in a three-tier model including RTI.* Bethesda, MD: National Association of School Psychologists.

Skalski, A. K., Minke, K., Rossen, E., Cowan, K. C., Kelly, J., Armistead, R., & Smith, A. (2015). NASP Practice Model Implementation Guide. Bethesda, MD: National Association of School Psychologists.

Skillstreaming (n. d.). Retrieved from http://www.skillstreaming.com/

Social academic instructional group curriculum. (n. d.). Retrieved from http://mps.milwaukee.k12.wi.us/ en/Families/Family-Services/Intervention---PBIS/SAIG-Curriculum.htm

Sprick, R. & Borgmeier, C. (2010). Behavior Prevention and Management in Three Tiers in Secondary Schools. In H. Walker & M. Shinn (Eds) *Interventions for Achievement and Behavior Problems in a Three-Tier Model Including RTI* (pp. 435 – 468).

Sullivan, A. L., & Long, L. (2010). Examining the changing landscape of school psychology practice: A survey of school-based practitioners regarding response to intervention. *Psychology in the Schools, 47*(10), 1059 – 1070. doi: 10.1002/pits.20524

Support for students exposed to trauma (n. d.). Retrieved from https://traumaawareschools.ort/sset

TEAMS/POD Intervention Team (2003). *The adolescent coping with stress course: Leader manual.* Retrieved from https://www.kpchr.org/research/public/common /getdocpublic.aspx?docid==2E11CCFD-84F5-47B5-9332-25B4A784F72E

The University of the State of New York & the State Education Department. (2010). *Response to intervention: Guidance for New York State School Districts.* Retrieved from http://www. p12.nysed.gov/biling/docs//RTIGuidance-Final11-10.pdf

Tibbets, T. J. (2013). *Identifying and assessing students with emotional disturbance.* Baltimore, Maryland: Paul H. Brooks Publishing Co., Inc.

Walker, B. (2009). A sample of commercially available screening tools that address social and behavioral domains. Retrieved from http://www.ndsec.org/2010connectionhandouts/ /PBIS%20Tier%202%20Training/screening_tools_table.pdf

Wayne County Regional Education Service Agency. (2004). Social maladjustment: A guide to differential diagnosis and educational options. Wayne, MI: Author. Retrieved from http://www.resa.net/downloads/special_education_guidelines?social_maladjustment.pdf

What is the SDQ? (n. d.). Retrieved from http://www.sdqinfo.com/a0.html

What is SWIS? (n. d.). Retrieved from http://nyspbis.org/SWIS/SWISintro.cfm

Wright, J. (n. d.). *Curriculum-based measurement: A manual for teachers.* Retrieved from http://www.jim Wrightonline.com/pdfdocs/cbaManual.pdf

Appendix

All MTSS flowcharts on the following page

**To learn more about preventative practice, provide a book review, obtain printouts, or report broken links, please visit:
http://geschaffer.wixsite.com/nutsandbolts

General Commonalities Across MTSS Domains

For additional resources and printouts visit: *http://geschaffer.wixsite.com/nutsandbolts*

Tiers *Figure 3*	Academics/RtI	Behavior/ SWPBIS	Social/ Emotional	Suicide Prevention
Tier 1 (80 – 85% of students)	1. Educate parents, staff, and students on general expectations and policies in attendance, academics, and behavior 2. Increase parents, staff, and students' awareness in social-emotional competency and suicide prevention 3. Create a warm, welcoming, and caring school environment that fosters and values academic, behavioral, and social-emotional growth. 4. Universally screen all students and analyze data across each of the 5 domains 5. Meet with child study team and school psychologist to determine best intervention options for students who are not responding to Tier 1 interventions 6. Refer students who are not responding to Tier 1 intervention to receive Tier 2 support in their area(s) of deficit			
Tier 2 (15 – 20% of students)	1. Re-teach key components of instruction, policy, and expectations 2. Provide supplemental interventions in push-in or pull-out small groups (3 -6 students) 3. Intervention groups typically held 3 to 5 times per week for 30 – 45 minutes 4. Collect progress monitoring data on a weekly or bi-weekly basis (for RtI 12 – 14 data points are recommended per intervention). 5. If student fails to respond to initial Tier 2 intervention(s), meet with CST team to update on student progress and determine alternative Tier 2 intervention(s) to remediate area(s) of deficit 6. If all Tier 2 intervention efforts area exhausted recommend child to receive Tier 3 supports			
Tier 3 1 – 5% of Students	1. Provide intensive intervention through small group (2 – 3 students) or individualized interventions 2. Provide interventions 5 times per week for 30 to 45 minutes 3. Collect progress monitoring data on a weekly basis 4. If student fails to respond to initial Tier 3 intervention efforts, meet with CST to update on student progress and determine alternative Tier 3 intervention(s) to remediate area(s) of deficit 5. If all Tier 3 intervention efforts are exhausted, discuss with CST team recommending the child for special education services, or if attendance related, determine if outside assistance is needed (calling CPS, filing a PINS etc.) 6. Establish a wraparound continuum of care through working with family and outside clinicians/agencies			

Attendance Flow Chart

Figure 4

For more on MTSS & attendance visit: http://www.attendanceworks.org/tools/schools/3-tiers-of-intervention/

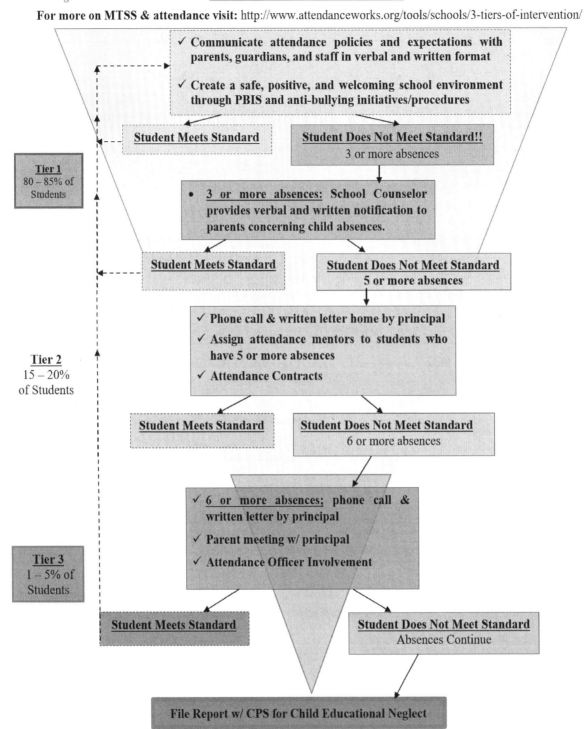

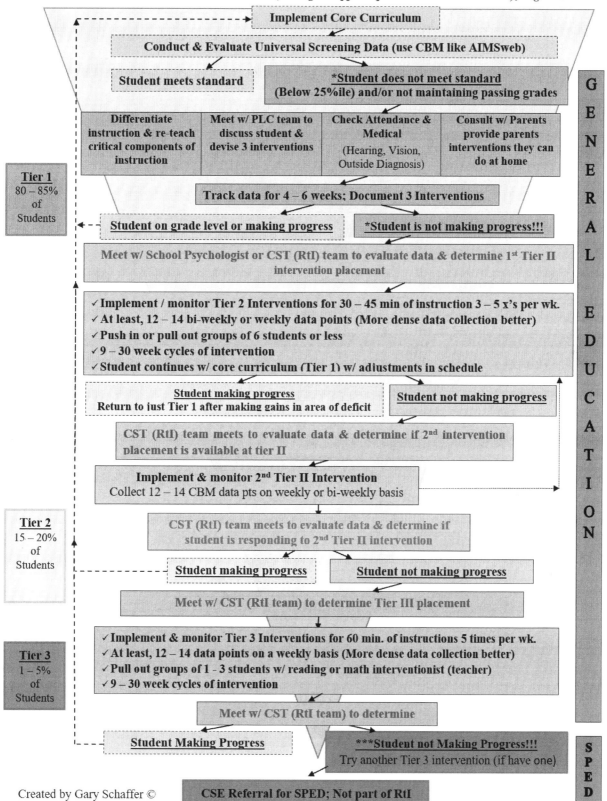

Implement Core Curriculum

Conduct & Evaluate Universal Screening Data (use CBM like AIMSweb)

Student meets standard

*Student does not meet standard
(Below 25%ile) and/or not maintaining passing grades

| Differentiate instruction & re-teach critical components of instruction | Meet w/ PLC team to discuss student & devise 3 interventions | Check Attendance & Medical (Hearing, Vision, Outside Diagnosis) | Consult w/ Parents provide parents interventions they can do at home |

Tier 1 80 – 85% of Students

Track data for 4 – 6 weeks; Document 3 Interventions

Student on grade level or making progress

*Student is not making progress!!!

Meet w/ School Psychologist or CST (RtI) team to evaluate data & determine 1st Tier II intervention placement

✓ Implement / monitor Tier 2 Interventions for 30 – 45 min of instruction 3 – 5 x's per wk.
✓ At least, 12 – 14 bi-weekly or weekly data points (More dense data collection better)
✓ Push in or pull out groups of 6 students or less
✓ 9 – 30 week cycles of intervention
✓ Student continues w/ core curriculum (Tier 1) w/ adjustments in schedule

Student making progress
Return to just Tier 1 after making gains in area of deficit

Student not making progress

CST (RtI) team meets to evaluate data & determine if 2nd intervention placement is available at tier II

Implement & monitor 2nd Tier II Intervention
Collect 12 – 14 CBM data pts on weekly or bi-weekly basis

Tier 2 15 – 20% of Students

CST (RtI) team meets to evaluate data & determine if student is responding to 2nd Tier II intervention

Student making progress

Student not making progress

Meet w/ CST (RtI team) to determine Tier III placement

✓ Implement & monitor Tier 3 Interventions for 60 min. of instructions 5 times per wk.
✓ At least, 12 – 14 data points on a weekly basis (More dense data collection better)
✓ Pull out groups of 1 - 3 students w/ reading or math interventionist (teacher)
✓ 9 – 30 week cycles of intervention

Tier 3 1 – 5% of Students

Meet w/ CST (RtI team) to determine

Student Making Progress

***Student not Making Progress!!!
Try another Tier 3 intervention (if have one)

Created by Gary Schaffer ©

CSE Referral for SPED; Not part of RtI

G E N E R A L   E D U C A T I O N

S P E D

Figure 11 **Behavior SWPBS Flow Chart**

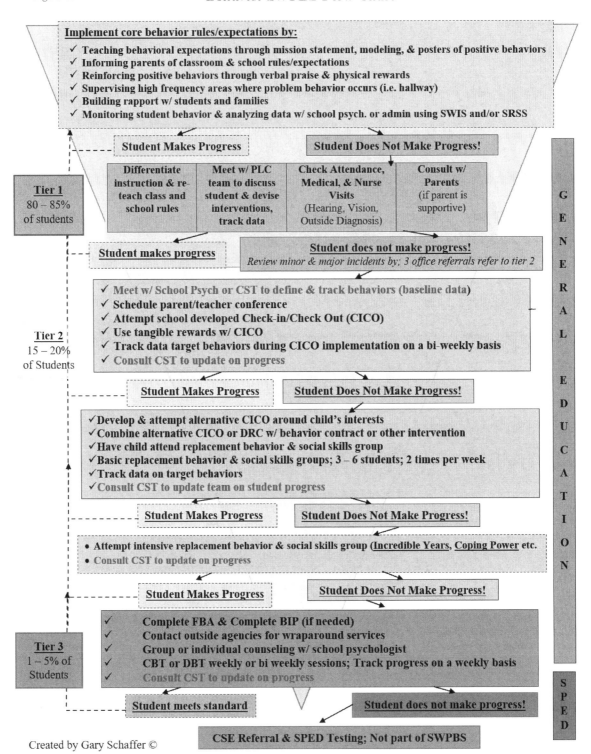

Implement core behavior rules/expectations by:
- ✓ Teaching behavioral expectations through mission statement, modeling, & posters of positive behaviors
- ✓ Informing parents of classroom & school rules/expectations
- ✓ Reinforcing positive behaviors through verbal praise & physical rewards
- ✓ Supervising high frequency areas where problem behavior occurs (i.e. hallway)
- ✓ Building rapport w/ students and families
- ✓ Monitoring student behavior & analyzing data w/ school psych. or admin using SWIS and/or SRSS

Student Makes Progress   **Student Does Not Make Progress!**

Tier 1
80 – 85% of students

| Differentiate instruction & re-teach class and school rules | Meet w/ PLC team to discuss student & devise interventions, track data | Check Attendance, Medical, & Nurse Visits (Hearing, Vision, Outside Diagnosis) | Consult w/ Parents (if parent is supportive) |

Student makes progress   **Student does not make progress!**
Review minor & major incidents by; 3 office referrals refer to tier 2

- ✓ Meet w/ School Psych or CST to define & track behaviors (baseline data)
- ✓ Schedule parent/teacher conference
- ✓ Attempt school developed Check-in/Check Out (CICO)
- ✓ Use tangible rewards w/ CICO
- ✓ Track data target behaviors during CICO implementation on a bi-weekly basis
- ✓ Consult CST to update on progress

Tier 2
15 – 20% of Students

Student Makes Progress   **Student Does Not Make Progress!**

- ✓ Develop & attempt alternative CICO around child's interests
- ✓ Combine alternative CICO or DRC w/ behavior contract or other intervention
- ✓ Have child attend replacement behavior & social skills group
- ✓ Basic replacement behavior & social skills groups; 3 – 6 students; 2 times per week
- ✓ Track data on target behaviors
- ✓ Consult CST to update team on student progress

Student Makes Progress   **Student Does Not Make Progress!**

- • Attempt intensive replacement behavior & social skills group (**Incredible Years**, **Coping Power** etc.
- • Consult CST to update on progress

Student Makes Progress   **Student Does Not Make Progress!**

Tier 3
1 – 5% of Students

- ✓ Complete FBA & Complete BIP (if needed)
- ✓ Contact outside agencies for wraparound services
- ✓ Group or individual counseling w/ school psychologist
- ✓ CBT or DBT weekly or bi weekly sessions; Track progress on a weekly basis
- ✓ Consult CST to update on progress

Student meets standard   **Student does not make progress!**

CSE Referral & SPED Testing; Not part of SWPBS

Created by Gary Schaffer ©

(Right side vertical text: GENERAL EDUCATION / SPED)

134

Figure 19

Social-Emotional Flow Chart

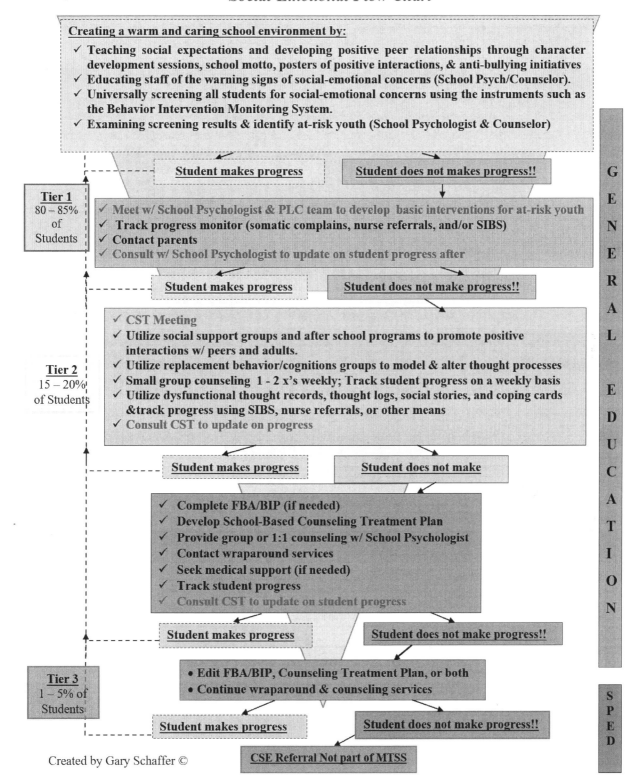

Creating a warm and caring school environment by:
- ✓ Teaching social expectations and developing positive peer relationships through character development sessions, school motto, posters of positive interactions, & anti-bullying initiatives
- ✓ Educating staff of the warning signs of social-emotional concerns (School Psych/Counselor).
- ✓ Universally screening all students for social-emotional concerns using the instruments such as the Behavior Intervention Monitoring System.
- ✓ Examining screening results & identify at-risk youth (School Psychologist & Counselor)

Student makes progress   **Student does not makes progress!!**

Tier 1
80 – 85% of Students
- ✓ Meet w/ School Psychologist & PLC team to develop basic interventions for at-risk youth
- ✓ Track progress monitor (somatic complains, nurse referrals, and/or SIBS)
- ✓ Contact parents
- ✓ Consult w/ School Psychologist to update on student progress after

Student makes progress   **Student does not make progress!!**

- ✓ CST Meeting
- ✓ Utilize social support groups and after school programs to promote positive interactions w/ peers and adults.
- ✓ Utilize replacement behavior/cognitions groups to model & alter thought processes
- ✓ Small group counseling 1 - 2 x's weekly; Track student progress on a weekly basis
- ✓ Utilize dysfunctional thought records, thought logs, social stories, and coping cards &track progress using SIBS, nurse referrals, or other means
- ✓ Consult CST to update on progress

Tier 2
15 – 20% of Students

Student makes progress   **Student does not make**

- ✓ Complete FBA/BIP (if needed)
- ✓ Develop School-Based Counseling Treatment Plan
- ✓ Provide group or 1:1 counseling w/ School Psychologist
- ✓ Contact wraparound services
- ✓ Seek medical support (if needed)
- ✓ Track student progress
- ✓ Consult CST to update on student progress

Student makes progress   **Student does not make progress!!**

Tier 3
1 – 5% of Students

- • Edit FBA/BIP, Counseling Treatment Plan, or both
- • Continue wraparound & counseling services

Student makes progress   **Student does not make progress!!**

CSE Referral Not part of MTSS

Created by Gary Schaffer ©

GENERAL EDUCATION

SPED

Figure 21   **Suicide Prevention and Intervention MTSS Flow Chart**

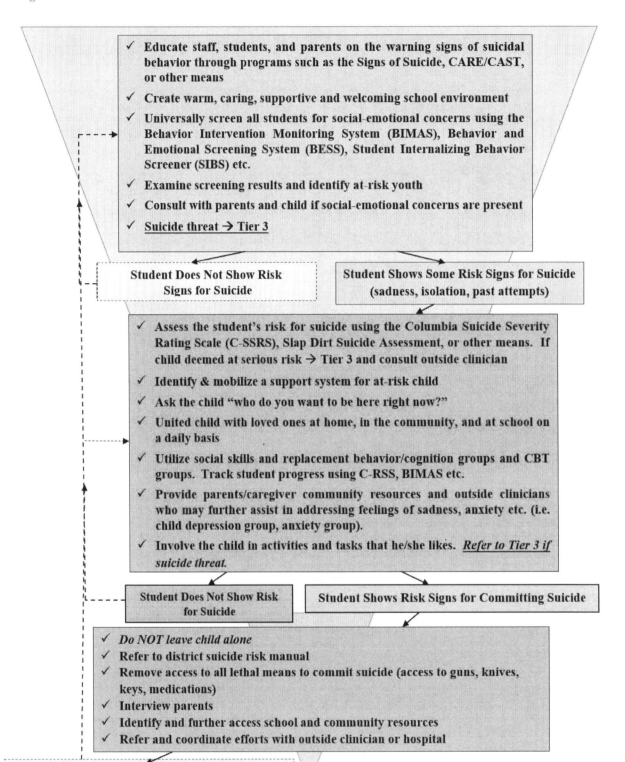

✓ Educate staff, students, and parents on the warning signs of suicidal behavior through programs such as the Signs of Suicide, CARE/CAST, or other means

✓ Create warm, caring, supportive and welcoming school environment

✓ Universally screen all students for social-emotional concerns using the Behavior Intervention Monitoring System (BIMAS), Behavior and Emotional Screening System (BESS), Student Internalizing Behavior Screener (SIBS) etc.

✓ Examine screening results and identify at-risk youth

✓ Consult with parents and child if social-emotional concerns are present

✓ <u>Suicide threat → Tier 3</u>

Student Does Not Show Risk Signs for Suicide

Student Shows Some Risk Signs for Suicide (sadness, isolation, past attempts)

✓ Assess the student's risk for suicide using the Columbia Suicide Severity Rating Scale (C-SSRS), Slap Dirt Suicide Assessment, or other means. If child deemed at serious risk → Tier 3 and consult outside clinician

✓ Identify & mobilize a support system for at-risk child

✓ Ask the child "who do you want to be here right now?"

✓ United child with loved ones at home, in the community, and at school on a daily basis

✓ Utilize social skills and replacement behavior/cognition groups and CBT groups. Track student progress using C-RSS, BIMAS etc.

✓ Provide parents/caregiver community resources and outside clinicians who may further assist in addressing feelings of sadness, anxiety etc. (i.e. child depression group, anxiety group).

✓ Involve the child in activities and tasks that he/she likes. *Refer to Tier 3 if suicide threat.*

Student Does Not Show Risk for Suicide

Student Shows Risk Signs for Committing Suicide

✓ *Do NOT leave child alone*

✓ Refer to district suicide risk manual

✓ Remove access to all lethal means to commit suicide (access to guns, knives, keys, medications)

✓ Interview parents

✓ Identify and further access school and community resources

✓ Refer and coordinate efforts with outside clinician or hospital

Work with outside clinician, administration, and parents to devise school re-entry plan when student is stable

Created by Gary Schaffer ©

Quick Access Video Playlist

1) *Introduction*

2) *What Areas Does MTSS Focus On?*

3) *Importance of Attendance*

4) *Commonalities of all MTSS Models*

5) *How Do MTSS Models Fail?*

6) *Patterns of Strengths and Weaknesses Model*

7) *Caveats to RtI*

8) *School-Wide Positive Behavior Support*

9) *Systematic Screening For Behavior Disorders*

10) *Importance of Children's Mental Health in School*

11) *Dialectical Behavior Therapy (DBT) in the School Setting*

12) *Cognitive Behavior Therapy (CBT) in the School Setting*

13) *Social-Emotional Progress Monitoring Using the BIMAS-2*

14) *Suicide Prevention & Intervention*

16) *Resource Allocation and MTSS*

17) *Role of the School Psychologist and MTSS*

18) *Final Thoughts*

Additional Resources

***To learn more about preventative practice, provide a book review, obtain printouts, or report broken links, please visit:
http://geschaffer.wixsite.com/nutsandbolts

<u>*NOTE ON ADDITIONAL RESOURCES FOR NUTS & BOLTS READERS:*</u>
- In the future, additional resources and content *may* be made available to those who have purchased this book at http://geschaffer.wixsite.com/nutsandbolts. Should additional resources become available on the site beyond what is available to the general viewing public (those who did not purchase the book), please enter the password *IPeP572Sp* in the member's section of the Nuts & Bolts website. Additionally, you may email the author to report broken links through the *Nuts & Bolts* website "contact" section.

80% of all proceeds for this book will be donated to the New York Association of School Psychologists (NYASP).

Thank you all for reading!

Please visit: http://geschaffer.wixsite.com/nutsandbolts.